MW01152489

# TABLE OF CONTENTS

# INTRODUCTION TO THE LSAT

The Law School Admission Test is a half-day standardized test required for admission to all ABA-approved law schools, most Canadian law schools, and many other law schools. It consists of five 35-minute sections of multiple-choice questions. Four of the five sections contribute to the test taker's score. These sections include one Reading Comprehension section, one Analytical Reasoning section, and two Logical Reasoning sections. The unscored section, commonly referred to as the variable section, typically is used to pretest new test questions or to preequate new test forms. The placement of this section in the LSAT will vary. A 35-minute writing sample is administered at the end of the test. The writing sample is not scored by LSAC, but copies are sent to all law schools to which you apply. The score scale for the LSAT is 120 to 180.

The LSAT is designed to measure skills considered essential for success in law school: the reading and comprehension of complex texts with accuracy and insight; the organization and management of information and the ability to draw reasonable inferences from it; the ability to think critically; and the analysis and evaluation of the reasoning and arguments of others.

The LSAT provides a standard measure of acquired reading and verbal reasoning skills that law schools can use as one of several factors in assessing applicants.

For up-to-date information about LSAC's services, go to our website, LSAC.org.

## SCORING

Your LSAT score is based on the number of questions you answer correctly (the raw score). There is no deduction for incorrect answers, and all questions count equally. In other words, there is no penalty for guessing.

### Test Score Accuracy—Reliability and Standard Error of Measurement

Candidates perform at different levels on different occasions for reasons quite unrelated to the characteristics of a test itself. The accuracy of test scores is best described by the use of two related statistical terms: reliability and standard error of measurement.

**Reliability** is a measure of how consistently a test measures the skills being assessed. The higher the reliability coefficient for a test, the more certain we can be that test takers would get very similar scores if they took the test again.

LSAC reports an internal consistency measure of reliability for every test form. Reliability can vary from 0.00 to 1.00, and a test with no measurement error would have a reliability coefficient of 1.00 (never attained in practice). Reliability coefficients for past LSAT forms have ranged from .90 to .95, indicating a high degree of consistency for these tests. LSAC expects the reliability of the LSAT to continue to fall within the same range.

LSAC also reports the amount of measurement error associated with each test form, a concept known as the standard error of measurement (SEM). The SEM, which is usually about 2.6 points, indicates how close a test taker's observed score is likely to be to his or her true score. True scores are theoretical scores that would be obtained from perfectly reliable tests with no measurement error—scores never known in practice.

Score bands, or ranges of scores that contain a test taker's true score a certain percentage of the time, can be derived using the SEM. LSAT score bands are constructed by adding and subtracting the (rounded) SEM to and from an actual LSAT score (e.g., the LSAT score, plus or minus 3 points). Scores near 120 or 180 have asymmetrical bands. Score bands constructed in this manner will contain an individual's true score approximately 68 percent of the time.

Measurement error also must be taken into account when comparing LSAT scores of two test takers. It is likely that small differences in scores are due to measurement error rather than to meaningful differences in ability. The standard error of score differences provides some guidance as to the importance of differences between two scores. The standard error of score differences is approximately 1.4 times larger than the standard error of measurement for the individual scores.

Thus, a test score should be regarded as a useful but approximate measure of a test taker's abilities as measured by the test, not as an exact determination of his or her abilities. LSAC encourages law schools to examine the range of scores within the interval that probably contains the test taker's true score (e.g., the test taker's score band) rather than solely interpret the reported score alone.

### Adjustments for Variation in Test Difficulty

All test forms of the LSAT reported on the same score scale are designed to measure the same abilities, but one test form may be slightly easier or more difficult than another. The scores from different test forms are made comparable through a statistical procedure known as equating. As a result of equating, a given scaled score earned on different test forms reflects the same level of ability.

### Research on the LSAT

Summaries of LSAT validity studies and other LSAT research can be found in member law school libraries and at LSAC.org.

## To Inquire About Test Questions

If you find what you believe to be an error or ambiguity in a test question that affects your response to the question, contact LSAC by e-mail: LSATTS@LSAC.org, or write to Law School Admission Council, Test Development Group, PO Box 40, Newtown, PA 18940-0040.

## HOW THIS PREPTEST DIFFERS FROM AN ACTUAL LSAT

This PrepTest is made up of the scored sections and writing sample from the actual disclosed LSAT administered in September 2016. However, it does not contain the extra, variable section that is used to pretest new test items of one of the three multiple-choice question types. The three multiple-choice question types may be in a different order in an actual LSAT than in this PrepTest. This is because the order of these question types is intentionally varied for each administration of the test.

## THE THREE LSAT MULTIPLE-CHOICE QUESTION TYPES

The multiple-choice questions that make up most of the LSAT reflect a broad range of academic disciplines and are intended to give no advantage to candidates from a particular academic background.

The five sections of the test contain three different question types. The following material presents a general discussion of the nature of each question type and some strategies that can be used in answering them.

### Analytical Reasoning Questions

Analytical Reasoning questions are designed to assess the ability to consider a group of facts and rules, and, given those facts and rules, determine what could or must be true. The specific scenarios associated with these questions are usually unrelated to law, since they are intended to be accessible to a wide range of test takers. However, the skills tested parallel those involved in determining what could or must be the case given a set of regulations, the terms of a contract, or the facts of a legal case in relation to the law. In Analytical Reasoning questions, you are asked to reason deductively from a set of statements and rules or principles that describe relationships among persons, things, or events.

Analytical Reasoning questions appear in sets, with each set based on a single passage. The passage used for each set of questions describes common ordering relationships or grouping relationships, or a combination of both types of relationships. Examples include scheduling employees for work shifts, assigning instructors to class sections, ordering tasks according to priority, and distributing grants for projects.

Analytical Reasoning questions test a range of deductive reasoning skills. These include:

- Comprehending the basic structure of a set of relationships by determining a complete solution to the problem posed (for example, an acceptable seating arrangement of all six diplomats around a table)

- Reasoning with conditional ("if-then") statements and recognizing logically equivalent formulations of such statements

- Inferring what could be true or must be true from given facts and rules

- Inferring what could be true or must be true from given facts and rules together with new information in the form of an additional or substitute fact or rule

- Recognizing when two statements are logically equivalent in context by identifying a condition or rule that could replace one of the original conditions while still resulting in the same possible outcomes

Analytical Reasoning questions reflect the kinds of detailed analyses of relationships and sets of constraints that a law student must perform in legal problem solving. For example, an Analytical Reasoning passage might describe six diplomats being seated around a table, following certain rules of protocol as to who can sit where. You, the test taker, must answer questions about the logical implications of given and new information. For example, you may be asked who can sit between diplomats X and Y, or who cannot sit next to X if W sits next to Y. Similarly, if you were a student in law school, you might be asked to analyze a scenario involving a set of particular circumstances and a set of governing rules in the form of constitutional provisions, statutes, administrative codes, or prior rulings that have been upheld. You might then be asked to determine the legal options in the scenario: what is required given the scenario, what is permissible given the scenario, and what is prohibited given the scenario. Or you might be asked to develop a "theory" for the case: when faced with an incomplete set of facts about the case, you must fill in the picture based on what is implied by the facts that are known. The problem could be elaborated by the addition of new information or hypotheticals.

No formal training in logic is required to answer these questions correctly. Analytical Reasoning questions are intended to be answered using knowledge, skills, and reasoning ability generally expected of college students and graduates.

## Suggested Approach

Some people may prefer to answer first those questions about a passage that seem less difficult and then those that seem more difficult. In general, it is best to finish one passage before starting on another, because much time can be lost in returning to a passage and reestablishing familiarity with its relationships. However, if you are having great difficulty on one particular set of questions and are spending too much time on them, it may be to your advantage to skip that set of questions and go on to the next passage, returning to the problematic set of questions after you have finished the other questions in the section.

Do not assume that because the conditions for a set of questions look long or complicated, the questions based on those conditions will be especially difficult.

**Read the passage carefully.** Careful reading and analysis are necessary to determine the exact nature of the relationships involved in an Analytical Reasoning passage. Some relationships are fixed (for example, P and R must always work on the same project). Other relationships are variable (for example, Q must be assigned to either team 1 or team 3). Some relationships that are not stated explicitly in the conditions are implied by and can be deduced from those that are stated (for example, if one condition about paintings in a display specifies that Painting K must be to the left of Painting Y, and another specifies that Painting W must be to the left of Painting K, then it can be deduced that Painting W must be to the left of Painting Y).

In reading the conditions, do not introduce unwarranted assumptions. For instance, in a set of questions establishing relationships of height and weight among the members of a team, do not assume that a person who is taller than another person must weigh more than that person. As another example, suppose a set involves ordering and a question in the set asks what must be true if both X and Y must be earlier than Z; in this case, do not assume that X must be earlier than Y merely because X is mentioned before Y. All the information needed to answer each question is provided in the passage and the question itself.

The conditions are designed to be as clear as possible. Do not interpret the conditions as if they were intended to trick you. For example, if a question asks how many people could be eligible to serve on a committee, consider only those people named in the passage unless directed otherwise. When in doubt, read the conditions in their most obvious sense. Remember, however, that the language in the conditions is intended to be read for precise meaning. It is essential to pay particular attention to words that describe or limit relationships, such as "only," "exactly," "never," "always," "must be," "cannot be," and the like.

The result of this careful reading will be a clear picture of the structure of the relationships involved, including the kinds of relationships permitted, the participants in the relationships, and the range of possible actions or attributes for these participants.

**Keep in mind question independence.** Each question should be considered separately from the other questions in its set. No information, except what is given in the original conditions, should be carried over from one question to another.

In some cases a question will simply ask for conclusions to be drawn from the conditions as originally given. Some questions may, however, add information to the original conditions or temporarily suspend or replace one of the original conditions for the purpose of that question only. For example, if Question 1 adds the supposition "if P is sitting at table 2 ...," this supposition should NOT be carried over to any other question in the set.

**Consider highlighting text and using diagrams.** Many people find it useful to underline key points in the passage and in each question. In addition, it may prove very helpful to draw a diagram to assist you in finding the solution to the problem.

In preparing for the test, you may wish to experiment with different types of diagrams. For a scheduling problem, a simple calendar-like diagram may be helpful. For a grouping problem, an array of labeled columns or rows may be useful.

Even though most people find diagrams to be very helpful, some people seldom use them, and for some individual questions no one will need a diagram. There is by no means universal agreement on which kind of diagram is best for which problem or in which cases a diagram is most useful. Do not be concerned if a particular problem in the test seems to be best approached without the use of a diagram.

## Logical Reasoning Questions

Arguments are a fundamental part of the law, and analyzing arguments is a key element of legal analysis. Training in the law builds on a foundation of basic reasoning skills. Law students must draw on the skills of analyzing, evaluating, constructing, and refuting arguments. They need to be able to identify what information is relevant to an issue or argument and what impact further evidence might have. They need to be able to reconcile opposing positions and use arguments to persuade others.

Logical Reasoning questions evaluate the ability to analyze, critically evaluate, and complete arguments as they occur in ordinary language. The questions are based on short arguments drawn from a wide variety of sources, including newspapers, general interest magazines, scholarly publications, advertisements, and informal discourse. These arguments mirror legal reasoning in the types of arguments presented and in their complexity, though few of the arguments actually have law as a subject matter.

Each Logical Reasoning question requires you to read and comprehend a short passage, then answer one question (or, rarely, two questions) about it. The questions are designed to assess a wide range of skills involved in thinking critically, with an emphasis on skills that are central to legal reasoning.

These skills include:

- Recognizing the parts of an argument and their relationships

- Recognizing similarities and differences between patterns of reasoning

- Drawing well-supported conclusions

- Reasoning by analogy

- Recognizing misunderstandings or points of disagreement

- Determining how additional evidence affects an argument

- Detecting assumptions made by particular arguments

- Identifying and applying principles or rules

- Identifying flaws in arguments

- Identifying explanations

The questions do not presuppose specialized knowledge of logical terminology. For example, you will not be expected to know the meaning of specialized terms such as "ad hominem" or "syllogism." On the other hand, you will be expected to understand and critique the reasoning contained in arguments. This requires that you possess a university-level understanding of widely used concepts such as argument, premise, assumption, and conclusion.

## Suggested Approach

Read each question carefully. Make sure that you understand the meaning of each part of the question. Make sure that you understand the meaning of each answer choice and the ways in which it may or may not relate to the question posed.

Do not pick a response simply because it is a true statement. Although true, it may not answer the question posed.

Answer each question on the basis of the information that is given, even if you do not agree with it. Work within the context provided by the passage. LSAT questions do not involve any tricks or hidden meanings.

## Reading Comprehension Questions

Both law school and the practice of law revolve around extensive reading of highly varied, dense, argumentative, and expository texts (for example, cases, codes, contracts, briefs, decisions, evidence). This reading must be exacting, distinguishing precisely what is said from what is not said. It involves comparison, analysis, synthesis, and application (for example, of principles and rules). It involves drawing appropriate inferences and applying ideas and arguments to new contexts. Law school reading also requires the ability to grasp unfamiliar subject matter and the ability to penetrate difficult and challenging material.

The purpose of LSAT Reading Comprehension questions is to measure the ability to read, with understanding and insight, examples of lengthy and complex materials similar to those commonly encountered in law school. The Reading Comprehension section of the LSAT contains four sets of reading questions, each set consisting of a selection of reading material followed by five to eight questions. The reading selection in three of the four sets consists of a single reading passage; the other set contains two related shorter passages. Sets with two passages are a variant of Reading Comprehension called Comparative Reading, which was introduced in June 2007.

Comparative Reading questions concern the relationships between the two passages, such as those of generalization/instance, principle/application, or point/counterpoint. Law school work often requires reading two or more texts in conjunction with each other and understanding their relationships. For example, a law student may read a trial court decision together with an appellate court decision that overturns it, or identify the fact pattern from a hypothetical suit together with the potentially controlling case law.

Reading selections for LSAT Reading Comprehension questions are drawn from a wide range of subjects in the humanities, the social sciences, the biological and physical sciences, and areas related to the law. Generally, the selections are densely written, use high-level vocabulary, and contain sophisticated argument or complex rhetorical structure (for example, multiple points of view). Reading Comprehension questions require you to read carefully and accurately, to determine the relationships among the various parts of the reading selection, and to draw reasonable inferences from the material in the selection. The questions may ask about the following characteristics of a passage or pair of passages:

- The main idea or primary purpose

- Information that is explicitly stated

- Information or ideas that can be inferred

- The meaning or purpose of words or phrases as used in context

- The organization or structure

- The application of information in the selection to a new context

- Principles that function in the selection

- Analogies to claims or arguments in the selection

- An author's attitude as revealed in the tone of a passage or the language used

- The impact of new information on claims or arguments in the selection

### Suggested Approach

Since reading selections are drawn from many different disciplines and sources, you should not be discouraged if you encounter material with which you are not familiar. It is important to remember that questions are to be answered exclusively on the basis of the information provided in the selection. There is no particular knowledge that you are expected to bring to the test, and you should not make inferences based on any prior knowledge of a subject that you may have. You may, however, wish to defer working on a set of questions that seems particularly difficult or unfamiliar until after you have dealt with sets you find easier.

**Strategies.** One question that often arises in connection with Reading Comprehension has to do with the most effective and efficient order in which to read the selections and questions. Possible approaches include:

- reading the selection very closely and then answering the questions;

- reading the questions first, reading the selection closely, and then returning to the questions; or

- skimming the selection and questions very quickly, then rereading the selection closely and answering the questions.

Test takers are different, and the best strategy for one might not be the best strategy for another. In preparing for the test, therefore, you might want to experiment with the different strategies and decide what works most effectively for you.

Remember that your strategy must be effective under timed conditions. For this reason, the first strategy—reading the selection very closely and then answering the questions—may be the most effective for you. Nonetheless, if you believe that one of the other strategies

might be more effective for you, you should try it out and assess your performance using it.

**Reading the selection.** Whatever strategy you choose, you should give the passage or pair of passages at least one careful reading before answering the questions. Try to distinguish main ideas from supporting ideas, and opinions or attitudes from factual, objective information. Note transitions from one idea to the next and identify the relationships among the different ideas or parts of a passage, or between the two passages in Comparative Reading sets. Consider how and why an author makes points and draws conclusions. Be sensitive to implications of what the passages say.

You may find it helpful to mark key parts of passages. For example, you might underline main ideas or important arguments, and you might circle transitional words—"although," "nevertheless," "correspondingly," and the like—that will help you map the structure of a passage. Also, you might note descriptive words that will help you identify an author's attitude toward a particular idea or person.

## Answering the Questions

- Always read all the answer choices before selecting the best answer. The best answer choice is the one that most accurately and completely answers the question being posed.

- Respond to the specific question being asked. Do not pick an answer choice simply because it is a true statement. For example, picking a true statement might yield an incorrect answer to a question in which you are asked to identify an author's position on an issue, since you are not being asked to evaluate the truth of the author's position but only to correctly identify what that position is.

- Answer the questions only on the basis of the information provided in the selection. Your own views, interpretations, or opinions, and those you have heard from others, may sometimes conflict with those expressed in a reading selection; however, you are expected to work within the context provided by the reading selection. You should not expect to agree with everything you encounter in Reading Comprehension passages.

## THE WRITING SAMPLE

On the day of the test, you will be asked to write one sample essay. LSAC does not score the writing sample, but copies are sent to all law schools to which you apply. According to a 2015 LSAC survey of 129 United States and Canadian law schools, almost all use the writing sample in evaluating at least some applications for admission. Failure to respond to writing sample prompts and frivolous responses have been used by law schools as grounds for rejection of applications for admission.

In developing and implementing the writing sample portion of the LSAT, LSAC has operated on the following premises: First, law schools and the legal profession value highly the ability to communicate effectively in writing. Second, it is important to encourage potential law students to develop effective writing skills. Third, a sample of an applicant's writing, produced under controlled conditions, is a potentially useful indication of that person's writing ability. Fourth, the writing sample can serve as an independent check on other writing submitted by applicants as part of the admission process. Finally, writing samples may be useful for diagnostic purposes related to improving a candidate's writing.

The writing prompt presents a decision problem. You are asked to make a choice between two positions or courses of action. Both of the choices are defensible, and you are given criteria and facts on which to base your decision. There is no "right" or "wrong" position to take on the topic, so the quality of each test taker's response is a function not of which choice is made, but of how well or poorly the choice is supported and how well or poorly the other choice is criticized.

The LSAT writing prompt was designed and validated by legal education professionals. Since it involves writing based on fact sets and criteria, the writing sample gives applicants the opportunity to demonstrate the type of argumentative writing that is required in law school, although the topics are usually nonlegal.

You will have 35 minutes in which to plan and write an essay on the topic you receive. Read the topic and the accompanying directions carefully. You will probably find it best to spend a few minutes considering the topic and organizing your thoughts before you begin writing. In your essay, be sure to develop your ideas fully, leaving time, if possible, to review what you have written. Do not write on a topic other than the one specified. Writing on a topic of your own choice is not acceptable.

No special knowledge is required or expected for this writing exercise. Law schools are interested in the reasoning, clarity, organization, language usage, and writing mechanics displayed in your essay. How well you write is more important than how much you write. Confine your essay to the blocked, lined area on the front and back of the separate Writing Sample Response Sheet. Only that area will be reproduced for law schools. Be sure that your writing is legible.

## TAKING THE PREPTEST UNDER SIMULATED LSAT CONDITIONS

One important way to prepare for the LSAT is to simulate the day of the test by taking a practice test under actual time constraints. Taking a practice test under timed conditions helps you to estimate the amount of time you can afford to spend on each question in a section and to determine the question types on which you may need additional practice.

Since the LSAT is a timed test, it is important to use your allotted time wisely. During the test, you may work only on the section designated by the test supervisor. You cannot devote extra time to a difficult section and make up that time on a section you find easier. In pacing yourself, and checking your answers, you should think of each section of the test as a separate minitest.

Be sure that you answer every question on the test. When you do not know the correct answer to a question, first eliminate the responses that you know are incorrect, then make your best guess among the remaining choices. Do not be afraid to guess as there is no penalty for incorrect answers.

When you take a practice test, abide by all the requirements specified in the directions and keep strictly within the specified time limits. Work without a rest period. When you take an actual test, you will have only a short break—usually 10–15 minutes—after SECTION III.

When taken under conditions as much like actual testing conditions as possible, a practice test provides very useful preparation for taking the LSAT.

Official directions for the four multiple-choice sections and the writing sample are included in this PrepTest so that you can approximate actual testing conditions as you practice.

To take the test:

- Set a timer for 35 minutes. Answer all the questions in SECTION I of this PrepTest. Stop working on that section when the 35 minutes have elapsed.

- Repeat, allowing yourself 35 minutes each for sections II, III, and IV.

- Set the timer again for 35 minutes, then prepare your response to the writing sample topic at the end of this PrepTest.

- Refer to "Computing Your Score" for the PrepTest for instruction on evaluating your performance. An answer key is provided for that purpose.

**The practice test that follows consists of four sections corresponding to the four scored sections of the September 2016 LSAT. Also reprinted is the September 2016 unscored writing sample topic.**

# General Directions for the LSAT Answer Sheet

The actual testing time for this portion of the test will be 2 hours 55 minutes. There are five sections, each with a time limit of 35 minutes. The supervisor will tell you when to begin and end each section. If you finish a section before time is called, you may check your work on that section **only;** do not turn to any other section of the test book and do not work on any other section either in the test book or on the answer sheet.

There are several different types of questions on the test, and each question type has its own directions. **Be sure you understand the directions for each question type before attempting to answer any questions in that section.**

Not everyone will finish all the questions in the time allowed. Do not hurry, but work steadily and as quickly as you can without sacrificing accuracy. You are advised to use your time effectively. If a question seems too difficult, go on to the next one and return to the difficult question after completing the section. **MARK THE BEST ANSWER YOU CAN FOR EVERY QUESTION. NO DEDUCTIONS WILL BE MADE FOR WRONG ANSWERS. YOUR SCORE WILL BE BASED ONLY ON THE NUMBER OF QUESTIONS YOU ANSWER CORRECTLY.**

**ALL YOUR ANSWERS MUST BE MARKED ON THE ANSWER SHEET.** Answer spaces for each question are lettered to correspond with the letters of the potential answers to each question in the test book. After you have decided which of the answers is correct, blacken the corresponding space on the answer sheet. **BE SURE THAT EACH MARK IS BLACK AND COMPLETELY FILLS THE ANSWER SPACE.** Give only one answer to each question. If you change an answer, be sure that all previous marks are **erased completely.** Since the answer sheet is machine scored, incomplete erasures may be interpreted as intended answers. **ANSWERS RECORDED IN THE TEST BOOK WILL NOT BE SCORED.**

There may be more question numbers on this answer sheet than there are questions in a section. Do not be concerned, but be certain that the section and number of the question you are answering matches the answer sheet section and question number. Additional answer spaces in any answer sheet section should be left blank. Begin your next section in the number one answer space for that section.

LSAC takes various steps to ensure that answer sheets are returned from test centers in a timely manner for processing. In the unlikely event that an answer sheet is not received, LSAC will permit the examinee either to retest at no additional fee or to receive a refund of his or her LSAT fee. **THESE REMEDIES ARE THE ONLY REMEDIES AVAILABLE IN THE UNLIKELY EVENT THAT AN ANSWER SHEET IS NOT RECEIVED BY LSAC.**

## Score Cancellation

Complete this section only if you are absolutely certain you want to cancel your score. **A CANCELLATION REQUEST CANNOT BE RESCINDED. IF YOU ARE AT ALL UNCERTAIN, YOU SHOULD NOT COMPLETE THIS SECTION.**

To cancel your score from this administration, you **must:**

**A.** fill in both ovals here ...... ◯ ◯
                    **AND**
**B.** read the following statement. Then sign your name and enter the date.
    **YOUR SIGNATURE ALONE IS NOT SUFFICIENT FOR SCORE CANCELLATION. BOTH OVALS ABOVE MUST BE FILLED IN FOR SCANNING EQUIPMENT TO RECOGNIZE YOUR REQUEST FOR SCORE CANCELLATION.**

**I certify that I wish to cancel my test score from this administration. I understand that my request is irreversible and that my score will not be sent to me or to the law schools to which I apply.**

Sign your name in full
_____

Date
_____

FOR LSAC USE ONLY  ⬤

## HOW DID YOU PREPARE FOR THE LSAT?
### (Select all that apply.)

**Responses to this item are voluntary and will be used for statistical research purposes only.**

◯ By studying the free sample questions available on LSAC's website.
◯ By taking the free sample LSAT available on LSAC's website.
◯ By working through official LSAT *PrepTests*, *ItemWise*, and/or other LSAC test prep products.
◯ By using LSAT prep books or software **not** published by LSAC.
◯ By attending a commercial test preparation or coaching course.
◯ By attending a test preparation or coaching course offered through an undergraduate institution.
◯ Self study.
◯ Other preparation.
◯ No preparation.

## CERTIFYING STATEMENT

Please write the following statement. Sign and date.

I certify that I am the examinee whose name appears on this answer sheet and that I am here to take the LSAT for the sole purpose of being considered for admission to law school. I further certify that I will neither assist nor receive assistance from any other candidate, and I agree not to copy, retain, or transmit examination questions in any form or discuss them with any other person.

_____
_____
_____
_____
_____
_____
_____

SIGNATURE: _____  TODAY'S DATE: ___ / ___ / ___
                                                                    MONTH  DAY  YEAR

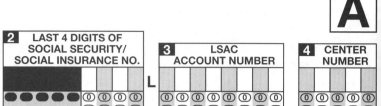

SCANTRON® EliteView™ EM-295665-1:654321

**A**

INSTRUCTIONS FOR COMPLETING THE BIOGRAPHICAL AREA ARE ON THE BACK COVER OF YOUR TEST BOOKLET.
**USE ONLY A NO. 2 OR HB PENCIL TO COMPLETE THIS ANSWER SHEET. DO NOT USE INK.**

**1** LAST NAME | FIRST NAME | MI

**2** LAST 4 DIGITS OF SOCIAL SECURITY/ SOCIAL INSURANCE NO.

**3** LSAC ACCOUNT NUMBER

**4** CENTER NUMBER

**5** DATE OF BIRTH
MONTH | DAY | YEAR
Jan, Feb, Mar, Apr, May, June, July, Aug, Sept, Oct, Nov, Dec

**6** TEST FORM CODE

**7** RACIAL/ETHNIC DESCRIPTION
**Mark one or more**
1 Amer. Indian/Alaska Na
2 Asian
3 Black/African America
4 Canadian Aboriginal
5 Caucasian/White
6 Hispanic/Latino
7 Native Hawaiian/ Other Pacific Islander
8 Puerto Rican
9 TSI/Aboriginal Austra

**8** SEX
Male
Female

**9** DOMINANT LANGUAGE
English
Other

**10** ENGLISH FLUENCY
Yes
No

**11** TEST DATE
MONTH / DAY / YEAR

**12** TEST FORM

## Law School Admission Test

Mark one and only one answer to each question. Be sure to fill in completely the space for your intended answer choice. If you erase, do so completely. Make no stray marks.

**13** TEST BOOK SERIAL NO.

| SECTION 1 | SECTION 2 | SECTION 3 | SECTION 4 | SECTION 5 |
|---|---|---|---|---|
| 1 A B C D E | 1 A B C D E | 1 A B C D E | 1 A B C D E | 1 A B C D E |
| 2 A B C D E | 2 A B C D E | 2 A B C D E | 2 A B C D E | 2 A B C D E |
| 3 A B C D E | 3 A B C D E | 3 A B C D E | 3 A B C D E | 3 A B C D E |
| 4 A B C D E | 4 A B C D E | 4 A B C D E | 4 A B C D E | 4 A B C D E |
| 5 A B C D E | 5 A B C D E | 5 A B C D E | 5 A B C D E | 5 A B C D E |
| 6 A B C D E | 6 A B C D E | 6 A B C D E | 6 A B C D E | 6 A B C D E |
| 7 A B C D E | 7 A B C D E | 7 A B C D E | 7 A B C D E | 7 A B C D E |
| 8 A B C D E | 8 A B C D E | 8 A B C D E | 8 A B C D E | 8 A B C D E |
| 9 A B C D E | 9 A B C D E | 9 A B C D E | 9 A B C D E | 9 A B C D E |
| 10 A B C D E | 10 A B C D E | 10 A B C D E | 10 A B C D E | 10 A B C D E |
| 11 A B C D E | 11 A B C D E | 11 A B C D E | 11 A B C D E | 11 A B C D E |
| 12 A B C D E | 12 A B C D E | 12 A B C D E | 12 A B C D E | 12 A B C D E |
| 13 A B C D E | 13 A B C D E | 13 A B C D E | 13 A B C D E | 13 A B C D E |
| 14 A B C D E | 14 A B C D E | 14 A B C D E | 14 A B C D E | 14 A B C D E |
| 15 A B C D E | 15 A B C D E | 15 A B C D E | 15 A B C D E | 15 A B C D E |
| 16 A B C D E | 16 A B C D E | 16 A B C D E | 16 A B C D E | 16 A B C D E |
| 17 A B C D E | 17 A B C D E | 17 A B C D E | 17 A B C D E | 17 A B C D E |
| 18 A B C D E | 18 A B C D E | 18 A B C D E | 18 A B C D E | 18 A B C D E |
| 19 A B C D E | 19 A B C D E | 19 A B C D E | 19 A B C D E | 19 A B C D E |
| 20 A B C D E | 20 A B C D E | 20 A B C D E | 20 A B C D E | 20 A B C D E |
| 21 A B C D E | 21 A B C D E | 21 A B C D E | 21 A B C D E | 21 A B C D E |
| 22 A B C D E | 22 A B C D E | 22 A B C D E | 22 A B C D E | 22 A B C D E |
| 23 A B C D E | 23 A B C D E | 23 A B C D E | 23 A B C D E | 23 A B C D E |
| 24 A B C D E | 24 A B C D E | 24 A B C D E | 24 A B C D E | 24 A B C D E |
| 25 A B C D E | 25 A B C D E | 25 A B C D E | 25 A B C D E | 25 A B C D E |
| 26 A B C D E | 26 A B C D E | 26 A B C D E | 26 A B C D E | 26 A B C D E |
| 27 A B C D E | 27 A B C D E | 27 A B C D E | 27 A B C D E | 27 A B C D E |
| 28 A B C D E | 28 A B C D E | 28 A B C D E | 28 A B C D E | 28 A B C D E |
| 29 A B C D E | 29 A B C D E | 29 A B C D E | 29 A B C D E | 29 A B C D E |
| 30 A B C D E | 30 A B C D E | 30 A B C D E | 30 A B C D E | 30 A B C D E |

**14** PLEASE PRINT INFORMATION

LAST NAME

FIRST NAME

DATE OF BIRTH

# THE PREPTEST

SECTION I

Time—35 minutes

26 Questions

Directions: The questions in this section are based on the reasoning contained in brief statements or passages. For some questions, more than one of the choices could conceivably answer the question. However, you are to choose the best answer; that is, the response that most accurately and completely answers the question. You should not make assumptions that are by commonsense standards implausible, superfluous, or incompatible with the passage. After you have chosen the best answer, blacken the corresponding space on your answer sheet.

1. After a major toll highway introduced a system of electronic toll paying, delays at all of its interchanges declined significantly. Travel time per car trip decreased by an average of 10 percent. Tailpipe pollution for each trip decreased commensurately. Despite this, the total air pollution from vehicles on that highway did not decrease measurably.

   Which one of the following, if true, most helps to resolve the apparent discrepancy in the information above?

   (A) The highway began charging higher tolls when it switched to electronic toll paying.

   (B) Even after the switch to electronic toll paying, there were sometimes long delays at the highway's interchanges.

   (C) The prospect of faster, more convenient travel induced more drivers to use the highway.

   (D) Travel time on the highway for car trips under 30 kilometers (18.6 miles) did not decrease appreciably.

   (E) Some drivers did not switch to the electronic system but instead continued to use cash to pay their tolls at toll booths.

2. A lack of trust in one's neighbors leads to their lack of respect for the law. A new study provides compelling evidence for this. Neighborhoods in which people routinely lock their doors have higher burglary rates than neighborhoods in which people do not routinely lock their doors.

   The reasoning in the argument is flawed in that the argument

   (A) treats something that is merely sufficient to produce a result as if it were necessary to produce that result

   (B) draws a moral conclusion from evidence that could only support a factual conclusion

   (C) bases its conclusion on data that are contradictory

   (D) asserts in a premise what it is trying to establish in its conclusion

   (E) treats what could be the effect of something as if it were the cause of that thing

3. In recent decades, government efforts to fight counterfeiting have been extremely successful, especially efforts to remove counterfeit bills from circulation. Yet counterfeiters are not finding it at all difficult to get away with passing counterfeit bills to merchants and even banks.

   Which one of the following, if true, most helps to resolve the apparent discrepancy in the information above?

   (A) Government information campaigns that teach merchants and bank tellers how to detect counterfeit bills are more effective than ever.

   (B) Governments are continually developing new currency designs with features that are difficult for criminals to counterfeit.

   (C) Counterfeiters are generally unaware that the percentage of fake bills in circulation is the lowest it has ever been.

   (D) Government success in removing counterfeit bills from circulation has caused merchants and bank tellers to become lax in checking for counterfeit bills.

   (E) Governments are spending larger and larger sums of money in their efforts to remove counterfeit bills from circulation.

GO ON TO THE NEXT PAGE.

4. If a civilization as technologically advanced as human civilization existed on another planet and that planet were within 50 light years of Earth, that civilization would have found evidence of intelligent life on Earth and could have easily contacted us. Scientists can thus rule out the possibility of finding a civilization as technologically advanced as our own within 50 light years of Earth.

Which one of the following is an assumption required by the argument?

(A) Scientists who are searching for evidence of extraterrestrial life forms generally focus their search on evidence of technologically advanced life forms.
(B) There is no reason to doubt the possibility that there are technologically advanced civilizations on planets more than 50 light years from Earth.
(C) If scientists received a message from a technologically advanced civilization on another planet, they would be able to decipher it fully.
(D) A technologically advanced civilization on another planet would want to communicate with intelligent life that it detected on Earth.
(E) Intelligent life forms on other planets would be able to recognize all signs of intelligent life on Earth.

5. Recently, many traffic lights and street markings were temporarily removed from a heavily traveled street in a major metropolitan area. Given that this street experiences significant volumes of automobile traffic, the number of accidents on the street was expected to increase. However, even though the street experienced no reduction in traffic, the number of accidents was greatly reduced.

Which one of the following, if true, most helps to resolve the apparent conflict described above?

(A) People often disregard traffic lights and street markings.
(B) The lack of traffic lights and street markings caused drivers to drive more cautiously.
(C) Most drivers were not aware that traffic lights and street markings had been removed.
(D) Traffic lights and street markings are intended to have benefits in addition to those related to safety.
(E) Drivers were given advance notice that the traffic lights and street markings would be removed.

6. Some have argued that body size influences mating decisions throughout all societies. Their argument rests largely on self-reports of university-age students and on analyses of personal advertisements in newspapers for dating partners.

The reasoning in the argument described above is most vulnerable to criticism on the grounds that the argument

(A) concludes that one kind of event causes another kind of event without ruling out the possibility that both kinds of events are the result of a third kind of event
(B) bases a conclusion on a sample that may be unrepresentative of the population about which the conclusion is drawn
(C) concludes that an effect has only one cause in the face of evidence that the effect has multiple causes
(D) uses a claim that applies only to entire societies to draw a conclusion about individual persons
(E) draws a universal conclusion on the basis of a very small number of individual cases

7. Journalist: The new mayor is undeniably bold. His assertions are made with utter certainty and confidence. While these kinds of assertions may make him popular with the public, they also demonstrate that he is not an introspective person.

Which one of the following is an assumption required by the journalist's argument?

(A) Introspective people do not make assertions with utter certainty and confidence.
(B) Politicians who make assertions with utter certainty and confidence are popular with the public.
(C) People who are bold make public assertions with utter certainty and confidence.
(D) People whose assertions are uncertain and lack confidence are introspective.
(E) Politicians who are not bold are unpopular with the public.

GO ON TO THE NEXT PAGE.

8. While studying a large colony of macaque monkeys, scientists interacting with baby monkeys under a week old found that the babies would imitate some, but not all, of the scientists' actions. The babies readily smacked their lips and stuck out their tongues when the scientists did, but stared impassively when the scientists opened and closed their mouths or made hand gestures. Of these four kinds of actions, only lip smacking and sticking out the tongue are used by adult macaques when interacting with babies.

The statements above, if true, most strongly support which one of the following?

(A)  Baby macaques under a week old are natural mimics of whatever they see.

(B)  Baby macaques under a week old cannot imitate hand gestures because they do not yet control the necessary muscles.

(C)  Adult macaques use lip smacking and sticking out the tongue to entertain infant macaques.

(D)  Baby macaques under a week old mistake the scientists interacting with them for adult macaques.

(E)  Baby macaques under a week old only imitate human gestures also used by adult macaques.

9. Some scientists believe that small humanoid skeletons found on an Indonesian island are the remains of human beings with a growth disorder. It is more likely that they represent a distinct human species that became smaller over time due to environmental pressure. These skeletons do not fit the pattern of known growth disorders. And evidence suggests that certain fox and mouse species on the island have evolved into smaller versions of their common counterparts.

Which one of the following most accurately expresses the conclusion drawn in the argument?

(A)  Some scientists believe that the humanoid skeletons are the remains of human beings with a growth disorder.

(B)  It is more likely that the humanoid skeletons represent a distinct human species than that they are the remains of human beings with a growth disorder.

(C)  The humanoid skeletons do not fit the pattern of known growth disorders.

(D)  Certain fox and mouse species on an Indonesian island have evolved into smaller versions of their common counterparts.

(E)  Environmental pressure can cause species living on islands to become smaller over time.

10. The more sunlight our planet reflects back into space, the cooler the global atmosphere tends to become. Snow and ice reflect much more sunlight back into space than do ocean water or land without snow cover. Therefore, the greater the area of Earth's surface that is covered with snow and ice, the cooler, on average, the global atmosphere is likely to become.

Which one of the following, if true, would most strengthen the argument?

(A)  Low atmospheric temperatures are required for the formation of clouds that result in snow.

(B)  Other factors besides the reflectivity of ice and snow affect the cooling of Earth's atmosphere.

(C)  Ocean water and land heated by sunlight in turn warm Earth's atmosphere.

(D)  The atmosphere derives most of its heat from the passage of sunlight through it.

(E)  Lighter-colored soil reflects more sunlight back into space than does darker-colored soil.

11. Nick: The Pincus family and their construction company have supported our university financially for decades. The university should not give the contract for building its new library to the family's main competitor. Doing so would be disloyal to a friend of the university.

Pedro: Accepting a donation does not oblige the university to give the donor any special privileges. If it did, then it wouldn't really be a charitable contribution. We should award the contract to whatever company makes the most competitive bid.

The dialogue provides the most support for the claim that Nick and Pedro disagree over whether

(A)  loyalty should sometimes be a consideration in making business decisions

(B)  the Pincus family and their construction company donated money for the purpose of acquiring special privileges from the university

(C)  the acceptance of donations places a university under a special obligation to the donor

(D)  the university should be more grateful to donors with a long history of financial support than to new donors

(E)  the Pincus family's construction company did not make the most competitive bid

GO ON TO THE NEXT PAGE.

12. Ampicillin and other modern antibiotics kill a much wider variety of bacteria than penicillin does. They also carry higher profit margins, so drug companies now have an incentive to stop manufacturing the older, less profitable antibiotics. This could cause a penicillin shortage, forcing doctors to use the much more powerful new antibiotics in cases where they might otherwise be unnecessary. Thus, these newer antibiotics are likely to result in an outbreak of diseases caused by drug-resistant bacteria, since _____.

The conclusion of the argument is most strongly supported if which one of the following completes the passage?

(A) drug-resistant bacteria flourish in the absence of competition from a wide variety of other bacteria
(B) older antibiotics like penicillin have been widely used for many decades
(C) a shortage of penicillin would drive up its price and profit margin
(D) treatment of diseases with the powerful new antibiotics is much more expensive than treatment with the older ones
(E) most bacteria that are resistant to penicillin are not resistant to ampicillin and other modern antibiotics

13. Weingarten claims that keeping animals in zoos is unethical. He points out that it involves placing animals in unnatural environments merely for the sake of human amusement. However, since Weingarten sees nothing wrong with owning pets, and keeping pets surely involves placing an animal in an unnatural environment merely for human amusement, his claim should be rejected.

The reasoning in the argument is flawed in that the argument

(A) takes for granted that Weingarten owns one or more pets
(B) inappropriately generalizes from a particular case
(C) misrepresents the conclusion of the opposing argument
(D) takes a necessary condition for a practice's being unethical as a sufficient condition for its being so
(E) rejects a claim merely on the grounds that its proponent holds another view inconsistent with it

14. Activist: President Zagel should resign, because she is unable to govern effectively given the widespread belief that she rigged the election.

President Zagel: Over the last decade, scandals have forced two presidents of this country to resign. If I were to resign, the rest of the world would see us as a country whose political system is hopelessly unstable. That would be unacceptable, so I must remain in office.

Which one of the following principles, if valid, most helps to justify the activist's argument in the face of President Zagel's argument?

(A) A country whose election procedures are resistant to illegitimate manipulation will eventually become politically stable.
(B) The leader of a country should resign if doing so is likely to improve that country's international reputation for political stability.
(C) If a president is involved in a scandal that is more serious than scandals that have forced previous leaders to resign, then that president should resign.
(D) If it can be conclusively proven that an officeholder rigged an election, then that officeholder should be removed from office.
(E) It is more important for a country to have a leader who can govern effectively than it is to be viewed by other countries as having a stable political system.

15. A popular book argues that people who are successful in business have, without exception, benefited from a lot of luck on their way to success. But this is ridiculous. Anyone who has studied successful people knows that success requires a lot of hard work.

The argument commits which one of the following errors of reasoning?

(A) It mistakes the claim that something is required for a purpose for the claim that it is sufficient for that purpose.
(B) It accepts a view as authoritative without establishing the authority of the source of the view.
(C) It takes for granted in a premise what it is trying to prove in its conclusion.
(D) It treats an effect of something as the cause of that thing.
(E) It attacks the source of an argument rather than attacking the substance of that argument.

GO ON TO THE NEXT PAGE.

16. University president: When a faculty member's falsification of research was uncovered, the media treated it as evidence of the university's low standards, even though in truth it was a mere case of dishonesty. But since vigilance with respect to academic standards is always necessary, it's good that standards have become a topic of discussion.

Which one of the following conforms most closely to the principle illustrated above?

(A) The latest government scandal was caused primarily by a lack of oversight, which in turn led to corruption. Since no amount of oversight can eliminate all corruption, it is important that the problems with oversight are not the only topic of discussion.

(B) The latest government scandal has been attributed to lack of oversight, although the true cause of the scandal was simple corruption. Nonetheless, this discussion of oversight is welcome, because oversight is important in its own right.

(C) The latest government scandal has been attributed to both lack of oversight and corruption. As a result, these important concerns are now being discussed. So, despite the harm that it caused, it is good that the scandal occurred.

(D) The latest government scandal has been analyzed as a case of simple corruption, although corruption had little to do with it. Because the true cause of the scandal was lack of oversight, attributing the cause of the scandal to simple corruption is harmful.

(E) The latest government scandal has been analyzed as a case of simple corruption, with no mention of the role played by lack of oversight. Nonetheless, the focus on corruption is welcome, because corruption played the largest role in the scandal.

17. Politician: Over the next decade, our city will be replacing all of its street signs with signs that are designed for improved readability. But since no one is complaining about the current signs, installing the new ones is a colossal waste of time and money.

Which one of the following would be most useful to know in evaluating the politician's argument?

(A) What features of the new street signs improve the readability of the signs?

(B) Are the new street signs considerably more expensive to manufacture than the current street signs were?

(C) What percentage of its street signs does the city replace annually in the course of ordinary maintenance?

(D) Do any other cities plan to replace their street signs with signs designed for improved readability?

(E) Were experts consulted when the new street signs were designed?

18. A large survey of scientists found that almost all accept Wang's Law, and almost all know the results of the Brown-Eisler Experiment. But those results together with Wang's Law contradict the Minsk Hypothesis. Therefore, most of the scientists surveyed reject the Minsk Hypothesis.

The argument requires assuming which one of the following?

(A) The scientists surveyed are generally aware that the results of the Brown-Eisler Experiment together with Wang's Law contradict the Minsk Hypothesis.

(B) The scientists in the survey who know the results of the Brown-Eisler Experiment are exactly the same ones who accept Wang's Law.

(C) Almost all of the scientists surveyed are familiar with the way in which the results of the Brown-Eisler Experiment were obtained.

(D) The sample is large enough to be representative of scientists in the field.

(E) Wang's Law has in fact been shown to be true.

GO ON TO THE NEXT PAGE.

19. Any literary translation is a compromise between two goals that cannot be entirely reconciled: faithfulness to the meaning of the text and faithfulness to the original author's style. Thus, even the most skillful translation will be at best a flawed approximation of the original work.

Which one of the following principles, if valid, most helps to justify the reasoning in the argument above?

(A) A translation of a literary work should be entirely faithful to neither the meaning of the text nor the original author's style.

(B) If a literary translation is flawed as an approximation of the original work, it cannot be regarded as a successful compromise between faithfulness to the meaning of the text and faithfulness to the original author's style.

(C) The most skillful literary translation of a work will not necessarily be the most balanced compromise between faithfulness to the meaning of the text and faithfulness to the original author's style.

(D) Any translation that is not entirely faithful to both the meaning of the text and the original author's style will be at best a flawed approximation of that work.

(E) Not even the most skillful literary translation could be faithful to both the literal meaning of the text and the original author's style.

20. Sociologist: Television, telephones, and other electronic media encourage imprecise, uncritical thinking. Yet critical thinking is the only adequate protection against political demagogues, who seek to exploit people by presenting emotionally loaded language as an objective description of reality.

If the sociologist's statements are true, then each of the following statements could be true EXCEPT:

(A) There are no political demagogues in some highly technological societies.

(B) Political demagogues are not the only ones who seek to exploit people by presenting emotionally loaded language as an objective description of reality.

(C) Highly emotional people are more easily exploited than less emotional people.

(D) The mere presence of an orderly system of government in a society provides adequate protection against political demagogues.

(E) The mere presence of electronic communications technology in a society provides adequate protection against the erosion of media freedoms.

21. People with higher-than-average blood levels of a normal dietary by-product called homocysteine are twice as likely to be diagnosed with Alzheimer's disease as are those with average or below-average homocysteine levels. Thus, it is likely that the risk of developing Alzheimer's disease could be reduced by including in one's diet large amounts of B vitamins and folic acid, which convert homocysteine into substances known to have no relation to Alzheimer's disease.

Which one of the following, if true, most seriously weakens the argument?

(A) Many Alzheimer's patients have normal homocysteine levels.

(B) The substances into which homocysteine is converted can sometimes have harmful effects unrelated to Alzheimer's disease.

(C) B vitamins and folic acid are not metabolized by the body very efficiently when taken in the form of vitamin-mineral supplements.

(D) People whose relatives contracted Alzheimer's disease are much more likely to develop Alzheimer's than those whose relatives did not.

(E) Alzheimer's disease tends to increase the levels of homocysteine in the blood.

22. Consumer advocate: Economists reason that price gouging—increasing the price of goods when no alternative seller is available—is efficient because it allocates goods to people whose willingness to pay more shows that they really need those goods. But willingness to pay is not proportional to need. In the real world, some people simply cannot pay as much as others. As a result, a price increase will allocate goods to the people with the most money, not to those with the most need.

Which one of the following most accurately describes the role played in the consumer advocate's argument by the claim that willingness to pay is not proportional to need?

(A) It disputes one explanation in order to make way for an alternative explanation.

(B) It is the overall conclusion of the argument.

(C) It is a component of reasoning disputed in the argument.

(D) It is a general principle whose validity the argument questions.

(E) It denies a claim that the argument takes to be assumed in the reasoning that it rejects.

GO ON TO THE NEXT PAGE.

23. Zoologist: Plants preferentially absorb heavy nitrogen from rainwater. Heavy nitrogen consequently becomes concentrated in the tissues of herbivores, and animals that eat meat in turn exhibit even higher concentrations of heavy nitrogen in their bodily tissues. We compared bone samples from European cave bears of the Ice Age with blood samples from present-day bears fed meat-enriched diets, and the levels of heavy nitrogen present in these samples were identical. Thus, the prehistoric European cave bears were not exclusively herbivores.

Which one of the following, if true, would most strengthen the zoologist's argument?

(A) Plants can also absorb heavy nitrogen from a variety of sources other than rainwater.

(B) The rate at which heavy nitrogen accumulated in the blood of Ice Age herbivores can be inferred from samples of their bones.

(C) The same number of samples was taken from present-day bears as was taken from Ice Age cave bears.

(D) Bone samples from present-day bears fed meat-enriched diets exhibit the same levels of heavy nitrogen as do their blood samples.

(E) The level of heavy nitrogen in the bones of any bear fed a meat-enriched diet is the same as that in the bones of any other meat-eating bear.

24. Biologist: Some computer scientists imagine that all that is required for making an artificial intelligence is to create a computer program that encapsulates the information contained in the human genome. They are mistaken. The operation of the human brain is governed by the interactions of proteins whose structures are encoded in the human genome.

Which one of the following is an assumption required by the biologist's argument?

(A) The functions of the human brain are governed by processes that cannot be simulated by a computer.

(B) The interactions of the proteins that govern the operation of the human brain are not determined by the information contained in the human genome.

(C) The only way to create an artificial intelligence is to model it on the operation of the human brain.

(D) The amount of information contained in the human genome is too large to be easily encapsulated by a computer program.

(E) It is much more difficult to write a program that encapsulates the interactions of proteins than to write a program that encapsulates the information contained in the human genome.

GO ON TO THE NEXT PAGE.

25. Some advertisers offer certain consumers home computers free of charge. Advertisements play continuously on the computers' screens whenever they are in use. As consumers use the computers to browse the Internet, information about their browsing patterns is sent to the advertisers, enabling them to transmit to each consumer advertising that accurately reflects his or her individual interests. The advertisers can afford to offer the computers for free because of the increased sales that result from this precise targeting of individual consumers.

Which one of the following is most strongly supported by the information above?

(A) At least some consumers who use a computer offered free of charge by advertisers for browsing the Internet spend more money on purchases from those advertisers than they would if they did not use such a computer to browse the Internet.

(B) No advertisers could offer promotions that give away computers free of charge if consumers never used those computers to browse the Internet.

(C) There are at least some consumers who browse the Internet using computers offered free of charge by the advertisers and who, if they did not use those computers to browse the Internet, would spend little if any money on purchases from those advertisers.

(D) The advertisers would not be able to offer the computers absolutely free of charge if advertisements that accurately reflected the interests of the computers' users did not play continuously across the computers' screens whenever they were in use.

(E) Consumers who use a computer offered free of charge by the advertisers can sometimes choose to abstain from having information about their browsing patterns sent to the advertisers.

26. Some eloquent speakers impress their audiences with the vividness and clarity of the messages conveyed. Speakers who resort to obscenity, however, are not genuinely eloquent, so none of these speakers impress their audiences.

The flawed reasoning in which one of the following is most similar to that in the argument above?

(A) A culture without myths will also lack fundamental moral certainties. Thus, this culture must lack fundamental moral certainties, since it is devoid of myth.

(B) There are authors who write one page a day and produce one book per year. Serious authors, however, do not write one page per day, so some authors who write one book a year are not serious.

(C) Cities that are centers of commerce are always centers of industry as well. It follows that some centers of commerce are small cities, since there are centers of industry that are not small cities.

(D) Most farmers like living in rural areas. Since Carla is not a farmer, she probably would not enjoy living in the country.

(E) Sculptors sometimes produce significant works of art. But musicians are not sculptors. Hence, musicians never produce significant works of art.

# S T O P
IF YOU FINISH BEFORE TIME IS CALLED, YOU MAY CHECK YOUR WORK ON THIS SECTION ONLY.
DO NOT WORK ON ANY OTHER SECTION IN THE TEST.

SECTION II

Time—35 minutes

27 Questions

Directions: Each set of questions in this section is based on a single passage or a pair of passages. The questions are to be answered on the basis of what is stated or implied in the passage or pair of passages. For some of the questions, more than one of the choices could conceivably answer the question. However, you are to choose the best answer; that is, the response that most accurately and completely answers the question, and blacken the corresponding space on your answer sheet.

**Passage A**

Muscle memory is a puzzling phenomenon. Most bodybuilders have experienced this phenomenon, yet virtually no discussions of it have appeared in scientific publications. Bodybuilders who start training
(5) again after a period of inactivity find that gaining muscle size seems easier the second time around— even if starting from the same place. With so many athletes observing muscle memory, some plausible explanation must exist.
(10) One potential explanation of muscle memory involves the neurons (nerve cells) that stimulate your muscles, telling the muscle fibers to contract. It is well established that during weight lifting, only a small percentage of neurons for the working muscles
(15) are recruited. The more weight you lift, the more neurons are involved and the more muscle fibers are stimulated. But even when attempting your maximum weight, you don't recruit all the fibers in your working muscles. Now it could be that one way your body
(20) adapts to the demands of consistent training is by gradually increasing the percentage of muscle fibers that are stimulated by neurons during maximal lifts. When you're making a comeback, this ability to recruit more muscle fibers may remain intact. If so,
(25) your muscles would start with a greater capacity to develop force. Although you may think you're starting from the same place, this greater strength would enable faster progress.
Then again, it's also possible that the ease of
(30) retraining has nothing to do with your muscles: it could all be in your head. The first time you trained, you didn't know how much you could lift. So you increased weight cautiously. When retraining, you already know you can handle increasing weight
(35) because you've done it before. So you are likely to add weight more rapidly. These more rapid weight increases produce quicker gains in strength and size.

**Passage B**

Pumping up is easier for people who have been buff before, and now scientists think they know
(40) why—muscles retain one aspect of their former fitness even as they wither from lack of use.
Because muscle cells are huge, more than one nucleus is needed for making the large amounts of the proteins that give muscles their strength. Previous
(45) research has demonstrated that with exercise, muscle cells get even bigger by merging with stem cells that are nested between them. The muscle cells incorporate the nuclei that previously belonged to the stem cells. Researchers had thought that when muscles atrophy,

(50) the extra cell nuclei are killed by a cell death program called apoptosis.
In a recent study, researchers regularly stimulated the leg muscles of mice over a two-week period, during which time the muscle cells gained nuclei and
(55) increased in size. The researchers then let the muscles rest. As the muscles atrophied, the cells deflated to about 40 percent of their bulked-up size, but the number of nuclei in the cells did not change. Since the extra nuclei don't die, they could be poised to make
(60) muscle proteins again, providing a type of muscle memory at the cellular level.

1. Both passages seek an answer to which one of the following questions?

   (A) Why are explanations in the field of exercise physiology so inconclusive?
   (B) What is the best way for bodybuilders to begin training again after a period of inactivity?
   (C) Why is building muscle easier for people who have done so in the past?
   (D) Is muscle memory a purely psychological phenomenon?
   (E) Is there a psychological basis for the increases in muscle size and strength that result from exercise?

2. Passage B, but not passage A, seeks to achieve its purpose by

   (A) questioning the reality of an alleged phenomenon
   (B) discussing the results of a recent scientific experiment
   (C) appealing to the reader's personal experience
   (D) considering the psychological factors involved in bodybuilding
   (E) speculating about the cause of an observed phenomenon

GO ON TO THE NEXT PAGE.

3.  Passage B, unlike passage A, suggests that the phenomenon of muscle memory might be due to

    (A)　muscle cells' ability to merge with stem cells
    (B)　the body's ability to adapt to consistent training
    (C)　psychological factors
    (D)　a cell death program known as apoptosis
    (E)　the neurons that stimulate muscles

4.  It can be inferred from the passages that the author of passage A

    (A)　is more certain than the author of passage B about the existence of muscle memory
    (B)　probably agrees with the author of passage B about the explanation for muscle memory
    (C)　was probably not aware of the scientific research that is described in passage B
    (D)　probably disagrees with the author of passage B about how muscle cells' nuclei affect muscle strength
    (E)　tends to be more skeptical than the author of passage B about conclusions drawn about one species on the basis of experiments involving another species

5.  Given the style and tone of each passage, which one of the following is most likely to correctly describe the expected audience of each passage?

    (A)　Passage A: skeptics of the phenomenon under discussion
    　　　Passage B: people with personal experience of the phenomenon under discussion
    (B)　Passage A: scientific researchers
    　　　Passage B: athletic trainers and coaches
    (C)　Passage A: athletes who work with a trainer
    　　　Passage B: people who pursue a fitness program on their own
    (D)　Passage A: bodybuilders
    　　　Passage B: a general audience
    (E)　Passage A: sports psychologists
    　　　Passage B: exercise physiologists

6.  The author of passage B would be most likely to hold which one of the following views about the characterization of muscle memory offered in the first sentence of passage A?

    (A)　It confirms that bodybuilders' experiences should not be accepted at face value.
    (B)　It reflects a dichotomy between athletes' experience and processes occurring at the cellular level of their muscles.
    (C)　It would not be accepted by most athletes who have started retraining after a period of inactivity.
    (D)　It is less apt now in light of recent research than it was before that research was conducted.
    (E)　It stems from a fundamental misunderstanding of the principles of exercise psychology.

7.  Which one of the following is explicitly mentioned in passage B but not in passage A?

    (A)　the condition of a person's muscles when that person begins retraining
    (B)　muscles' adaptation to exercise
    (C)　the percentage of muscle fibers used in a working muscle
    (D)　the prevalence of discussions of muscle memory in scientific publications
    (E)　the large amounts of protein responsible for muscles' strength

GO ON TO THE NEXT PAGE.

Best known for her work with lacquer, Eileen Gray (1878–1976) had a fascinating and multifaceted artistic career: she became a designer of ornaments, furniture, interiors, and eventually homes.

(5) Though her attention shifted from smaller objects to the very large, she always focused on details, even details that were forever hidden. In Paris she studied the Japanese tradition of lacquer, employing wood surfaces—e.g., bowls, screens, furniture—for the

(10) application of the clear, hard-drying liquid. It is a time-consuming craft, then little known in Europe, that superimposes layer upon layer, sometimes involving twenty layers or more. The tradition of lacquer fit well with her artistic sensibilities, as Gray eschewed the

(15) flowing, leafy lines of the Art Nouveau movement that had flourished in Paris, preferring the austere beauty of straight lines and simple forms juxtaposed.

In addition to requiring painstaking layering, the wood used in lacquer work must be lacquered on both

(20) sides to prevent warping. This tension between aesthetic demands and structural requirements, which invests Gray's work in lacquer with an architectural quality, is critical but not always apparent: a folding screen or door panel reveals more of the artist's work

(25) than does a flat panel, which hides one side. In Gray's early work she produced flat panels; later she made door panels and even unfolded the panels into screens. In a screen she made for the lobby of an apartment, she fully realizes the implications of this expansion

(30) from two to three dimensions: the screen juts out from a wall, and that wall visually disintegrates into panels of lacquered bricks on the screen. The screen thus becomes a painting, a piece of furniture, and an architectural element all at once. She subsequently

(35) became heavily invested in the design of furniture, often tailoring pieces to fit a particular interior environment. She often used modern materials, such as tubular steel, to create furniture and environments that, though visually austere, meet their occupants' needs.

(40) Gray's work in both lacquer and interior design prefigures her work as an architect. She did not believe that one should divorce the structural design of the exterior from the design of the interior. She designed the interior elements of a house together with the

(45) more permanent structures, as an integrated whole. Architecture for her was like work in lacquer: it could only be achieved from the inside out. But in architecture we discover the hidden layers; in fact we inhabit them. We find storage cabinets in the recesses

(50) of a staircase, desks that are also cabinets, and tables that are set on pivots to serve different functions in different contexts. One such table can be positioned either outside, on a balcony, or inside the house. Gray placed a carpet underneath it in each location,

(55) as though to underscore that there is no important distinction between exterior and interior.

8. Which one of the following most accurately summarizes the main point of the passage?

(A) Eileen Gray's artistic career, which ranged from interior to exterior design, was greatly influenced by her early work in lacquer, which molded her aesthetic sensibilities and caused her to develop independence as an artist, yet prevented her from garnering acclaim by critics of contemporary art.

(B) Eileen Gray's artistic career, ranging from the design of ornaments and interiors to architectural design, was exemplified by her work in lacquer, from which she derived an aesthetic that downplayed the distinctions between interior and exterior and sought integral wholeness in a work of art.

(C) Eileen Gray, a multifaceted artist whose designs ranged from ornaments to houses, is best known for her use of modern materials such as tubular steel in the design of furniture and houses, which, while informed by an austerity of line, create humanistic environments that meet their occupants' needs.

(D) Although Eileen Gray's artistic endeavors ranged from the design of ornaments and interiors to architectural design, her distinctive style, which is characterized by a sense of the hidden, is evident in all her work, making it readily identifiable.

(E) The fact that Eileen Gray's artistic career evolved from the design of ornaments and furniture to architecture ultimately derives from her eventual dissatisfaction with Japanese traditional art and its emphasis on integral wholeness.

9. Which one of the following comes closest to exemplifying the characteristics of Gray's work as described in the passage?

(A) an upholstered sofa with tasseled fringes and curved, wooden arms

(B) a coffee table decorated with intricate carvings of birds, trees, and grasses that are painted in bright colors

(C) a thin, stainless steel vase intended to resemble the ornate flowers it will hold

(D) a round, wooden picture frame inlaid with glass beads, pearls, and gracefully cut pieces of colorful shells

(E) a metal chair whose simple shape is adapted to fit the human form

GO ON TO THE NEXT PAGE.

10. The passage provides information that most strongly supports which one of the following assertions?

    (A) Gray's reputation rests primarily on the range of styles and media in which she worked, rather than on her work in any particular medium.

    (B) Gray personally constructed most of the interior furnishings that she designed.

    (C) In Paris in Gray's time, wood was generally considered an inappropriate medium for visual art.

    (D) Few of Gray's works in lacquer were intended for public viewing.

    (E) Much of Gray's later work was functional as well as ornamental.

11. Information in the passage most helps to answer which one of the following questions?

    (A) When did the tradition of lacquer first become known in Europe?

    (B) What types of wood are usually considered best for use in traditional Japanese lacquer work?

    (C) Were the artistic motifs of traditional lacquer work similar to those that were typical of Art Nouveau?

    (D) Did Gray allow the style of her architecture to be informed by the landscape that surrounded the building site?

    (E) What is a material that Gray used both structurally for its superior strength and decoratively for its visual interaction with another material?

12. Which one of the following most accurately characterizes the author's attitude toward Gray's artistic accomplishments?

    (A) appreciation of the fact that her aesthetic philosophy, as well as the materials she used and the range of her work, sets her work apart from that of many of her contemporaries

    (B) admiration for her artistic independence and refusal to conform to contemporary art trends even though such refusal positioned her on the periphery of the art world

    (C) appreciation for the interpretation of Japanese tradition in her work, by which she made a unique contribution to modern architectural design while remaining faithful to Japanese architectural traditions

    (D) admiration for the rapid development in her career, from the production of smaller works, such as ornaments, to large structures, like houses, that ensured her reputation as an avant-garde artist

    (E) appreciation for her help in revolutionizing the field of structural design through her use of traditional materials and modern materials in her furniture creations and architectural work

13. The passage most strongly suggests that which one of the following principles was used by Gray in her work?

    (A) Traditional lacquering techniques can be applied to nontraditional materials, such as brick and steel, with artistically effective results.

    (B) The nature and placement of a dwelling's interior features can be essential factors in determining the overall structural design of the dwelling.

    (C) Traditional ornamental techniques that are usually applied to small items are especially suitable for use on large structural elements of buildings.

    (D) Excellent artistic effects can be achieved through the juxtaposition of visually austere elements with gracefully ornate elements of design.

    (E) The superficial visual aspects of a building's decor can give evidence of the materials that have been used in its basic, unseen structural components.

14. The passage most strongly suggests that the author would agree with which one of the following statements about Gray's architectural work?

    (A) It was considered by other architects of her time to be iconoclastic and inconsistent with sound principles of structural design.

    (B) Her involvement in it was marked by a radical shift in her attitude toward the relation between the expressive and functional aspects of her work.

    (C) The public is less knowledgeable about it than about at least some of her other work.

    (D) It has been less controversial among recent critics and scholars than has at least some of her work in interior design.

    (E) Unlike her work in lacquer, it was not influenced by an established tradition of Asian art.

GO ON TO THE NEXT PAGE.

It is generally accepted that woodland clearings were utilized by Mesolithic human populations (populations in Europe roughly 7,000 to 12,000 years ago) for food procurement. Whether there was
(5) deliberate removal of tree cover to attract grazing animals or whether naturally created clearings just afforded opportunistic hunting, the common view is that clearings had an economic use. The archaeological evidence for this, however, is at best circumstantial.
(10) Some locales where the presence of clearings has been demonstrated in the paleoecological record of vegetation have also yielded human artifacts from around the same time, but the two kinds of evidence are never securely linked. Furthermore, artifactual
(15) evidence that preparation of animals for human consumption took place within or near such clearings is generally lacking.

Most of the evidence invoked in favor of the resource-procurement model for clearings comes from
(20) ethnography rather than archaeology, and principally from the recognition that some recent premodern populations used fire to increase grazing areas. But while some ethnographic evidence has been used to bolster the resource-procurement model, other
(25) ethnographic evidence may suggest a different vision, a noneconomic one, of why clearings may have been deliberately created and/or used.

Geographer Yi-Fu Tuan argues that right up through the modern era, human behavior has been
(30) driven by fear of the wilderness. While we might be tempted to see this kind of anxiety as a product of modern urban life, it is clear that such fears are also manifest in preliterate and nonurban societies. If we apply this insight to the Mesolithic era, our view of the
(35) purpose and use of woodland clearings may change.

We have recently become aware of the importance of woodland paths in prehistory. The fact that Mesolithic human populations moved around the landscape is not a new idea. However, the fact that
(40) they may have done so along prescribed pathways has only recently come to the fore. I propose that one of the primary motivators in establishing paths may have been fear of the wooded surroundings—whether fear of harm from wildlife or spirits, or of simply
(45) getting lost.

From this view an alternative hypothesis may be developed. First, paths become established and acquire a measure of long-term permanence. Then this permanence leads to concentration of activity in some
(50) areas (near the paths) rather than others (away from the paths). This allows us to legitimately consider wilderness as a motivating concept in the Mesolithic, and may force us to consider environment as more than "backdrop." And finally, it may lead us to
(55) explain some clearings as purely social phenomena, since where paths meet, wider clearings emerge as corners are cut and intersections become convenient spots for resting.

15. Which one of the following most accurately states the main idea of the passage?

(A) Though fear of the wilderness is commonly thought to be a modern urban phenomenon, archaeological evidence suggests that the concept of wilderness may go as far back as the Mesolithic period.

(B) Though the resource-procurement model for Mesolithic woodland clearings is widely accepted, the available evidence provides comparable support for an alternative, noneconomic model.

(C) Though ethnographic evidence appears to support the resource-procurement model for woodland clearings, archaeological evidence suggests that clearings were used for multiple purposes by Mesolithic human populations.

(D) Evidence of woodland clearings from the paleoecological record of plant types may lend support to the hypothesis that Mesolithic human populations moved around the landscape via established paths.

(E) Ethnography provides clear and unambiguous insight into the purpose and use of woodland clearings during the Mesolithic period.

16. According to the resource-procurement model for clearings, Mesolithic human populations engaged in which one of the following practices?

(A) They traveled on preestablished pathways.
(B) They hunted animals that grazed in clearings.
(C) They grazed domesticated animals in clearings.
(D) They used clearings as resting sites.
(E) They planted crops in clearings.

17. Which one of the following is most clearly an example of the kind of evidence that would lend support to the author's proposal in the next-to-last paragraph?

(A) Mesolithic artwork that appears to depict woodland paths and clearings

(B) the ubiquity of paths and roads in areas densely settled by humans

(C) maps showing pathways used by certain recent premodern human populations

(D) survey results showing that modern urban dwellers experience heightened anxiety in wilderness areas

(E) rituals performed by certain recent premodern populations for the purpose of protection in the forest

GO ON TO THE NEXT PAGE.

18. The author suggests that which one of the following may have been true of Mesolithic human populations?

    (A)   They were the first people to use fire to increase grazing areas.
    (B)   They were the first people to travel in prescribed pathways.
    (C)   They worshipped nature.
    (D)   They possessed a concept of wilderness.
    (E)   They had a complex economic system.

19. In the third paragraph, the author mentions Yi-Fu Tuan's argument primarily in order to

    (A)   render doubtful the hypothesis about clearings that the author seeks to challenge
    (B)   exemplify the kind of argument about clearings that the author seeks to challenge
    (C)   give credit to the scholar who developed the hypothesis about clearings that the author favors
    (D)   lay the groundwork for the hypothesis about clearings that the author outlines
    (E)   point out the similarity between Tuan's view about clearings and the author's view

20. It can be inferred that the author would be more likely to endorse the resource-procurement model for clearings if this model were supported by which one of the following kinds of evidence?

    (A)   artifactual evidence that it was near or within clearings that Mesolithic human populations processed animals for human consumption
    (B)   ethnographic evidence that certain recent premodern populations used clearings for resource procurement
    (C)   experimental evidence that the creation of clearings is an effective means of attracting grazing animals
    (D)   paleoecological evidence that the majority of woodland clearings during the Mesolithic period were the result of wildfires
    (E)   statistical evidence that there was a significant increase in the number of woodland clearings during the Mesolithic period

21. Which one of the following comes closest to capturing what the phrase "purely social phenomena" means in line 55?

    (A)   phenomena that arise as by-products of a society's noneconomic practices
    (B)   phenomena that are universal and unique to human societies
    (C)   phenomena that serve the purpose of strengthening ties between a society's members
    (D)   phenomena that are intentionally created by human actions to produce a social benefit
    (E)   phenomena that reveal information about a society's cultural and economic development

22. Which one of the following arguments is most closely analogous to the author's argument in the second paragraph?

    (A)   The prosecution's case against the defendant rests almost entirely on circumstantial evidence. The defense, in contrast, has provided direct evidence that establishes that the defendant could not have committed the crime in question.
    (B)   The prosecution maintains that the physical evidence presented establishes the defendant's guilt. However, that same physical evidence can be interpreted in such a way that it instead establishes the defendant's innocence.
    (C)   The prosecution's case against the defendant rests entirely on circumstantial evidence. This suggests that there is no direct evidence to support the charge against the defendant.
    (D)   The prosecution's primary witness against the defendant is known to be untrustworthy. The defense, in contrast, has provided a parade of witnesses whose reputations are beyond reproach.
    (E)   The prosecution's case against the defendant rests almost entirely on circumstantial evidence. However, there is other circumstantial evidence that suggests that the defendant is innocent.

GO ON TO THE NEXT PAGE.

A remedy that courts sometimes use in disputes involving a breach of contract is simply to compel the participants in the contract to do precisely what they have agreed to do. Specific performance, as this
(5) approach is called, can be used as an alternative to monetary damages—that is, to requiring the one who has violated the agreement to pay a specified amount of money in compensation for the loss that is incurred or the wrong that is suffered. But while there are some
(10) cases for which specific performance can be a better alternative than monetary damages, there are many instances in which it is clearly not a suitable remedy.

Whether or not specific performance is an appropriate remedy in a case depends on the particular
(15) characteristics of that case. It is often the only reasonable remedy when monetary damages could not adequately compensate the one who has been harmed by the breach of contract. For example, a contract may provide for one party to sell some item of personal
(20) property that is unique or of such subjective importance to the buyer that there is no way to assign an accurate financial measure of the buyer's loss in not possessing the item. When the promised seller in such a case refuses to complete the sale, the best remedy would be
(25) to order that the contract be fulfilled exactly according to its terms.

Nevertheless, in many cases monetary payment can adequately compensate for the refusal to fulfill the terms of a contract, and thus the court commonly need
(30) not consider ordering specific performance. In fact, in some types of cases, court-enforced performance of the contract would actually be detrimental to those involved in the dispute and thus should be avoided. This most often occurs when a contract calls for a
(35) service to be performed and the one who has previously agreed to perform the service now refuses to do so— especially if a contract has been broken through someone's refusal to undertake employment as promised. The most compelling reasons against
(40) enforcement of contracts in such cases have to do with the kind of coercion that enforcement would necessitate. Forcing someone to perform a service in association with, and especially under the direction of, another who has become an antagonist can, at the very
(45) least, heighten dissatisfaction and intensify psychological friction. Even if a court had the resources necessary to ensure that such a contract would be enforced according to its terms, it would often do better to avoid imposing such uncomfortable
(50) conditions. Awarding monetary compensation where possible in such cases permits the court to steer clear of entanglement in troublesome aspects of the disputed relationship while still providing relief to the wronged party.

23. Based on the information in the passage, which one of the following is most clearly an example of a court's ordering specific performance?

(A) A publishing house is ordered by a court to return a manuscript to a writer after it has broken its contract for publication of the manuscript, and the contract has subsequently been nullified.
(B) A systems analyst who refuses to work for a certain company as she has contracted to do is ordered by a court to assume her contracted duties with the company, and the company is ordered to pay her the contracted salary.
(C) A building contractor who has received the full payment specified in his contract with a developer for the construction of a new mall but fails to complete the project is ordered to transfer all of the funds to a new contractor who will complete the construction.
(D) A dealer in rare antique furniture is ordered to return a contracted buyer's down payment for a chair after an expert appraiser has informed the buyer and the court that the chair's authenticity is questionable.
(E) An engineer who has agreed to work for a certain company but no longer intends to do so is ordered to pay the company for the losses it will incur as a result of the breach of agreement, but the company is not ordered to compensate the engineer.

24. Based on the passage, the author would be most likely to agree with which one of the following statements regarding cases in which someone is deemed by the court to have failed to undertake employment as contracted?

(A) Often specific performance in such cases can help the courts avoid problematic involvement in difficult aspects of the cases.
(B) While specific performance costs the court less to enforce than monetary damages, the savings should be weighed against the former's negative psychological repercussions.
(C) Enforcement of specific performance by the courts in such cases would often be less than fully successful.
(D) If the person who failed to fulfill the contract also refuses to pay monetary damages, specific performance should be imposed instead.
(E) Specific performance is more often considered by the courts in such cases than in other cases involving someone's refusal to perform services.

GO ON TO THE NEXT PAGE.

25. The main purpose of the passage is to

(A) predict the consequences of following a policy whereby a particular legal remedy becomes the standard approach

(B) argue for the implementation of a set of standards for the use of a new legal measure

(C) explain the differences among a group of interrelated legal procedures

(D) generate a set of guidelines for the evaluation of evidence in a particular type of legal dispute

(E) identify some criteria for the application of two different legal remedies

26. The passage most strongly suggests that the author would agree with which one of the following statements?

(A) Courts should examine the suitability of assessing monetary damages in breach-of-contract cases before they consider ordering specific performance.

(B) Specific performance is usually the most appropriate remedy for violations of contracts to sell personal property.

(C) In general, coercive court-ordered remedies in contract violation cases are unfair and should be avoided.

(D) Specific performance is successful at resolving disputes only when the objective value of the personal property contracted for sale is reasonably low.

(E) To provide fair enforcement of contracts, legal systems should offer disputing parties the option to use any of a number of resolution methods.

27. Which one of the following would, if true, most strengthen the author's position with regard to remedies in employment contract cases?

(A) Court-ordered compensation in employment cases is often nearly impossible to enforce.

(B) All types of court-ordered remedies for contract violations entail coercion of one or more of the parties involved in the dispute.

(C) Most people who are sued for violating their agreement to undertake employment have adequate financial resources to compensate their would-be employers.

(D) The legal issues involved in employment contract disputes are for the most part very different from the legal issues involved in other disputes over contracts for performance of services.

(E) The rights of potential employees often override the monetary considerations involved in employment contract disputes.

# S T O P

IF YOU FINISH BEFORE TIME IS CALLED, YOU MAY CHECK YOUR WORK ON THIS SECTION ONLY.
DO NOT WORK ON ANY OTHER SECTION IN THE TEST.

SECTION III

Time—35 minutes

23 Questions

Directions: Each group of questions in this section is based on a set of conditions. In answering some of the questions, it may be useful to draw a rough diagram. Choose the response that most accurately and completely answers each question and blacken the corresponding space on your answer sheet.

Questions 1–5

In one week—Monday through Friday—a library's bookmobile will visit five of the following six neighborhoods— Hidden Hills, Lakeville, Nottingham, Oldtown, Park Plaza, and Sunnyside. Exactly one neighborhood will be visited on each of the five days, and none of the neighborhoods will be visited on more than one day. The bookmobile's schedule must conform to the following conditions:

Hidden Hills is visited, but not on Friday.
If Oldtown is visited, then it is visited on the day immediately before Hidden Hills is visited.
If Lakeville is visited, then it is visited on Wednesday.
Nottingham and Sunnyside are both visited, but not on consecutive days.

1. The five neighborhoods visited by the bookmobile, listed in order from Monday through Friday, could be

   (A)   Nottingham, Lakeville, Oldtown, Hidden Hills, and Sunnyside
   (B)   Nottingham, Oldtown, Hidden Hills, Sunnyside, and Park Plaza
   (C)   Oldtown, Hidden Hills, Lakeville, Nottingham, and Sunnyside
   (D)   Sunnyside, Oldtown, Lakeville, Hidden Hills, and Nottingham
   (E)   Sunnyside, Park Plaza, Nottingham, Oldtown, and Hidden Hills

GO ON TO THE NEXT PAGE.

2.  Which one of the following neighborhoods CANNOT
    be visited on Thursday?

    (A)    Hidden Hills
    (B)    Nottingham
    (C)    Oldtown
    (D)    Park Plaza
    (E)    Sunnyside

3.  If Hidden Hills is visited on Monday, which one of the
    following must be true?

    (A)    Lakeville is visited on Wednesday.
    (B)    Nottingham is visited on Tuesday.
    (C)    Park Plaza is visited on Thursday.
    (D)    Sunnyside is visited on Tuesday.
    (E)    Sunnyside is visited on Friday.

4.  If Hidden Hills is visited on Wednesday, which one of
    the following must be true?

    (A)    Nottingham is visited on Monday.
    (B)    Oldtown is visited on Tuesday.
    (C)    Park Plaza is visited on Friday.
    (D)    Sunnyside is visited on Monday.
    (E)    Sunnyside is visited on Thursday.

5.  If Nottingham is visited on Thursday, which one of the
    following must be true?

    (A)    Hidden Hills is visited on Wednesday.
    (B)    Lakeville is visited on Wednesday.
    (C)    Oldtown is visited on Monday.
    (D)    Park Plaza is visited on Friday.
    (E)    Sunnyside is visited on Tuesday.

GO ON TO THE NEXT PAGE.

Questions 6–12

Six park rangers—Jefferson, Koguchi, Larson, Mendez, Olsen, and Pruitt—are each to be assigned to monitor one of three areas—area 1, area 2, and area 3—in a national park. At least one ranger, but no more than three, is assigned to each area. The assignment must conform to the following conditions:

Mendez is assigned to area 3.
Neither Olsen nor Pruitt is assigned to area 1.
Larson is assigned to the same area as either Koguchi or Mendez but not to the same area as both.
If Olsen is assigned to area 2, then Jefferson is assigned to the same area as Koguchi; otherwise, Jefferson is assigned to a different area than Koguchi.

6. Which one of the following is a permissible assignment of rangers to park areas?

(A) area 1: Jefferson, Koguchi
   area 2: Larson, Olsen
   area 3: Mendez, Pruitt
(B) area 1: Koguchi, Larson
   area 2: Olsen, Pruitt
   area 3: Jefferson, Mendez
(C) area 1: Koguchi, Pruitt
   area 2: Jefferson
   area 3: Larson, Mendez, Olsen
(D) area 1: Jefferson, Koguchi, Larson
   area 2: Mendez, Olsen
   area 3: Pruitt
(E) area 1: Jefferson, Koguchi, Larson
   area 2: Olsen, Pruitt
   area 3: Mendez

GO ON TO THE NEXT PAGE.

7. If Olsen is the sole ranger assigned to area 2, then which one of the following could be the complete assignment of rangers to area 3?

   (A) Mendez
   (B) Larson, Mendez
   (C) Mendez, Pruitt
   (D) Jefferson, Koguchi, Mendez
   (E) Jefferson, Mendez, Pruitt

8. If exactly one ranger is assigned to area 1, then which one of the following must be true?

   (A) Jefferson is assigned to area 1.
   (B) Koguchi is assigned to area 2.
   (C) Larson is assigned to area 3.
   (D) Olsen is assigned to area 3.
   (E) Pruitt is assigned to area 2.

9. Which one of the following rangers CANNOT be assigned to area 3?

   (A) Pruitt
   (B) Olsen
   (C) Larson
   (D) Koguchi
   (E) Jefferson

10. If Koguchi is assigned to area 2, then which one of the following could be true?

    (A) Jefferson is assigned to area 2.
    (B) Jefferson is assigned to area 3.
    (C) Larson is assigned to area 1.
    (D) Olsen is assigned to area 2.
    (E) Pruitt is assigned to area 3.

11. If Larson and Olsen are assigned to the same area, then which one of the following could be true?

    (A) Jefferson is assigned to area 3.
    (B) Koguchi is assigned to area 2.
    (C) Larson is assigned to area 1.
    (D) Olsen is assigned to area 2.
    (E) Pruitt is assigned to area 3.

12. If Jefferson is assigned to area 2, then which one of the following must be true?

    (A) Koguchi is assigned to area 1.
    (B) Larson is assigned to area 1.
    (C) Olsen is assigned to area 2.
    (D) Pruitt is assigned to area 2.
    (E) Pruitt is assigned to area 3.

GO ON TO THE NEXT PAGE.

**3**

Questions 13–17

An economics department is assigning six teaching assistants—
Ramos, Smith, Taj, Vogel, Yi, and Zane—to three courses—
Labor, Markets, and Pricing. Each assistant will be assigned
to exactly one course, and each course will have at least one
assistant assigned to it. The assignment of assistants to
courses is subject to the following conditions:

Markets must have exactly two assistants assigned to it.
Smith and Taj must be assigned to the same course as
 each other.
Vogel and Yi cannot be assigned to the same course as
 each other.
Yi and Zane must both be assigned to Pricing if either
 one of them is.

13. Which one of the following could be the complete
 assignment of assistants to Pricing?

(A)  Ramos, Yi, and Zane
(B)  Smith, Taj, and Yi
(C)  Smith, Taj, Yi, and Zane
(D)  Taj, Yi, and Zane
(E)  Vogel, Yi, and Zane

GO ON TO THE NEXT PAGE.

14. Which one of the following CANNOT be the complete assignment of assistants to Labor?

   (A)   Ramos, Vogel
   (B)   Ramos, Zane
   (C)   Smith, Taj
   (D)   Vogel, Zane
   (E)   Yi, Zane

15. Which one of the following could be true?

   (A)   Ramos and Vogel are both assigned to Markets.
   (B)   Ramos and Taj are both assigned to Markets.
   (C)   Smith and Vogel are both assigned to Markets.
   (D)   Smith and Zane are both assigned to Pricing.
   (E)   Vogel and Zane are both assigned to Pricing.

16. If Vogel is assigned to the same course as Zane, which one of the following CANNOT be true?

   (A)   Ramos is assigned to Labor.
   (B)   Smith is assigned to Labor.
   (C)   Taj is assigned to Markets.
   (D)   Ramos is assigned to Pricing.
   (E)   Smith is assigned to Pricing.

17. If no other assistant is assigned to the same course as Ramos, which one of the following must be true?

   (A)   Taj is assigned to Labor.
   (B)   Vogel is assigned to Labor.
   (C)   Yi is assigned to Markets.
   (D)   Zane is assigned to Markets.
   (E)   Smith is assigned to Pricing.

GO ON TO THE NEXT PAGE.

Questions 18–23

There are exactly six computers—P, Q, R, S, T, and U—
on a small network. Exactly one of those computers was
infected by a virus from outside the network, and that virus
was then transmitted between computers on the network.
Each computer received the virus exactly once. The following
pieces of information concerning the spread of the virus have
been established:

   No computer transmitted the virus to more than two other
      computers on the network.
   S transmitted the virus to exactly one other computer on
      the network.
   The computer that transmitted the virus to R also
      transmitted it to S.
   Either R or T transmitted the virus to Q.
   Either T or U transmitted the virus to P.

18. One possible route of the virus from the first computer
    in the network infected to Q is

    (A)    from R to P to T to Q
    (B)    from T to S to R to Q
    (C)    from T to S to U to Q
    (D)    from U to P to R to Q
    (E)    from U to T to P to R to Q

GO ON TO THE NEXT PAGE.

19. Which one of the following could be the computer that was infected from outside the network?

    (A) P
    (B) Q
    (C) R
    (D) S
    (E) T

20. If T did not transmit the virus to any other computer on the network, which one of the following must be true?

    (A) P transmitted the virus to S.
    (B) Q transmitted the virus to R.
    (C) U transmitted the virus to S.
    (D) P did not transmit the virus to any other computer on the network.
    (E) R did not transmit the virus to any other computer on the network.

21. Any of the following computers could have transmitted the virus to two other computers on the network EXCEPT:

    (A) P
    (B) Q
    (C) R
    (D) T
    (E) U

22. The spread of the virus among the computers is completely determined if which one of the following is true?

    (A) R transmitted the virus to Q.
    (B) T transmitted the virus to Q.
    (C) T transmitted the virus to S.
    (D) U transmitted the virus to P.
    (E) U transmitted the virus to R.

23. If P is the only computer that transmitted the virus to two other computers on the network, which one of the following must be true?

    (A) S transmitted the virus to T.
    (B) T transmitted the virus to P.
    (C) Q did not transmit the virus to any other computer on the network.
    (D) R did not transmit the virus to any other computer on the network.
    (E) U did not transmit the virus to any other computer on the network.

# S  T  O  P

IF YOU FINISH BEFORE TIME IS CALLED, YOU MAY CHECK YOUR WORK ON THIS SECTION ONLY.
DO NOT WORK ON ANY OTHER SECTION IN THE TEST.

SECTION IV

Time—35 minutes

25 Questions

Directions: The questions in this section are based on the reasoning contained in brief statements or passages. For some questions, more than one of the choices could conceivably answer the question. However, you are to choose the <u>best</u> answer; that is, the response that most accurately and completely answers the question. You should not make assumptions that are by commonsense standards implausible, superfluous, or incompatible with the passage. After you have chosen the best answer, blacken the corresponding space on your answer sheet.

1. Cool weather typically weakens muscle power in cold-blooded creatures. In the veiled chameleon, a cold-blooded animal, the speed at which the animal can retract its tongue declines dramatically as the temperature falls. However, the speed at which this chameleon can extend its tongue does not decline much as the temperature falls.

    Which one of the following, if true, most helps to resolve the apparent discrepancy in the information above?

    (A)    Most cold-blooded animals are much more active in warmer weather than in cooler weather.
    (B)    Many cold-blooded animals, including the veiled chameleon, have tongues that can extend quite a distance.
    (C)    Veiled chameleons are found in a wide range of habitats, including ones with wide variations in temperature and ones with moderate climates.
    (D)    In the veiled chameleon, tongue retraction is powered by muscles, whereas tongue extension is driven by energy stored in a rubber band-like sheath.
    (E)    Compared with the muscles in the tongues of most cold-blooded animals, the retraction muscles in the veiled chameleon's tongue are considerably stronger.

2. Acme's bank loan must be immediately repaid in full if Acme's earnings fall below $1 million per year. If Acme has to repay the entire loan immediately, it will have to declare bankruptcy. Acme had seemed safe from bankruptcy, having reported annual earnings of well over $1 million in each year it has had the bank loan. However, Acme has now admitted overstating its earnings for last year, so it will have to declare bankruptcy.

    The argument requires the assumption that

    (A)    Acme's earnings for last year, when accurately stated, are below $1 million
    (B)    Acme has other debts besides the bank loan
    (C)    last year is not the only year for which Acme overstated earnings
    (D)    Acme's earnings for the current year will fall below $1 million
    (E)    Acme would be able to avoid bankruptcy if it did not have to repay the bank loan

3. Hospital patients generally have lower infection rates and require shorter hospital stays if they are housed in private rooms rather than semiprivate rooms. Yet in Woodville's hospital, which has only semiprivate rooms, infection rates and length of stays are typically the same as in several nearby hospitals where most of the rooms are private, even though patients served by these hospitals are very similar to those served by Woodville's hospital.

    Which one of the following, if true, most helps to resolve the apparent conflict in the information above?

    (A)    Many of the doctors who routinely treat patients in Woodville's hospital also routinely treat patients in one or more of the nearby hospitals.
    (B)    Most of the nearby hospitals were built within the last 10 years, whereas Woodville's hospital was built about 50 years ago.
    (C)    Infection is more likely to be spread where people come into close contact with one another than where they do not.
    (D)    Woodville's hospital has a policy of housing one patient per room in semiprivate rooms whenever possible.
    (E)    Woodville's hospital is located in its central business district, whereas most of the nearby hospitals are located outside their municipalities' business districts.

GO ON TO THE NEXT PAGE.

4. Economist: Unemployment will soon decrease. If total government spending significantly increases next year, the economy will be stimulated in the short term and unemployment will decrease. If, on the other hand, total government spending significantly decreases next year, businesses will retain more of their earnings in the short term and employ more workers, thereby decreasing unemployment.

The conclusion drawn by the economist is properly inferred if which one of the following is assumed?

(A) Either total government spending will significantly decrease next year or else total government spending will significantly increase next year.

(B) Government officials are currently implementing policies that are intended to reduce unemployment.

(C) If there is a significantly increased demand for workers, then there will be a significant decrease in unemployment.

(D) A significant increase in total government spending will slow the economy in the long run.

(E) If the economy is not stimulated and businesses do not retain more of their earnings, then unemployment will not decrease.

5. Marisa: Existing zoning regulations must be loosened; in some places the restrictions on development are now so prohibitive as to reduce the property values of undeveloped areas significantly.

Tyne: I disagree. Though it is true that the recent increase in the stringency of zoning regulations could be seen by developers as merely an activists' ploy to restrict development further, the value of natural, undisturbed areas can only be better preserved by such regulatory protection.

Tyne's response to Marisa suggests that Tyne has misinterpreted which one of the following words in Marisa's remarks?

(A) regulations
(B) development
(C) prohibitive
(D) values
(E) significantly

6. Scientist: Laboratory animals have access to ample food, and they get relatively little exercise. These factors can skew the results of research using animals, since such studies often rely on the assumption that the animal subjects are healthy. For instance, animal studies that purport to show that extreme caloric restriction can extend lifespans take for granted that their subjects were not overfed to begin with.

The scientist's argument requires assuming which one of the following?

(A) Laboratory animals are healthy if they are fed a carefully restricted diet and get plenty of exercise.

(B) Laboratory conditions that provide animals with ample food but relatively little exercise can be unhealthy for the animals.

(C) It is not unusual for animals outside of laboratory settings to have access to ample food and get relatively little exercise.

(D) Some animal studies take into consideration the differences between the living conditions of laboratory animals and those of other animals.

(E) When provided with unlimited food over a long period of time, animals show little day-to-day variation in their eating habits.

7. Trade negotiator: Increasing economic prosperity in a country tends to bring political freedom to its inhabitants. Therefore, it is wrong for any country to adopt trade policies that are likely to seriously hinder growth in the prosperity of any other country.

Which one of the following principles, if valid, would most help to justify the trade negotiator's reasoning?

(A) Every country should adopt at least some policies that encourage the development of political freedom in other countries.

(B) Both economic prosperity and political freedom can contribute to the overall well-being of any country's inhabitants.

(C) The primary reason that any country seeks economic prosperity is to foster political freedom in that country.

(D) A country should not do anything that might hinder the growth of political freedom in any other country.

(E) It is wrong for any country to adopt trade policies that might diminish the prosperity of its inhabitants.

GO ON TO THE NEXT PAGE.

8. Whenever an artist endowed with both a high level of artistic skill and a high degree of creativity combines these two abilities in the process of creating an artwork, the resulting product is a great work of art. Moreover, no work of art can be great unless both of these elements are combined in its execution. Thus, great works of art are necessarily rare.

Which one of the following is an assumption required by the argument?

(A) Not every artist possesses a high level of artistic skill.
(B) A high degree of creativity and a high level of artistic skill are seldom combined in the creation of a work of art.
(C) An artist endowed with a high degree of creativity and a high level of artistic skill will necessarily produce great works of art.
(D) Few artists are endowed with a high degree of creativity.
(E) Anyone endowed with both a high level of artistic skill and a high degree of creativity will produce only a few great works of art.

9. Cereal advertisement: Fitness experts say that regular exercise is the most effective way to become physically fit, and studies have shown that adults who eat cereal every day exercise more regularly than adults who do not eat cereal. So by eating Fantastic Flakes every morning, you too will be on the most effective path to physical fitness.

The argumentation in the advertisement is flawed in that it

(A) infers a cause from a mere correlation
(B) presumes, without providing justification, that Fantastic Flakes are more nutritious than other cereals
(C) infers that a given factor is the sole predictor of a result merely on the grounds that the factor has been shown to contribute to that result
(D) draws a conclusion about all adults from a sample that is too small to be representative
(E) infers that some members of a group have a particular characteristic merely from the fact that the group as a whole has it

10. Journalist: Some critics argue that as the entertainment value of news reporting increases, the caliber of that reporting decreases. Yet the greatest journalists have been the most entertaining. So these critics are mistaken.

The journalist's conclusion is properly drawn if which one of the following is assumed?

(A) The news reporting of the greatest journalists has been of the highest caliber.
(B) The greatest journalists have been entertainers who report the news.
(C) Journalistic greatness involves producing news that is very valuable in some sense.
(D) Entertainment and news are not mutually exclusive categories.
(E) The worst journalists have been more entertaining than informative.

11. Linguist: Three of the four subfamilies of the so-called "Austronesian" languages are found only among indigenous peoples in Taiwan, whereas the fourth is found on islands over a huge area stretching from Madagascar to the eastern Pacific Ocean. Since these subfamilies all originated in the same language, which must have been originally spoken in a single geographic location, these facts suggest that Taiwan is the homeland where Austronesian languages have been spoken longest and, hence, that Austronesian-speaking peoples originated in Taiwan and later migrated to other islands.

Which one of the following most accurately expresses the overall conclusion drawn in the linguist's argument?

(A) The Austronesian family of languages has four subfamilies, three of which are found only among indigenous peoples in Taiwan.
(B) Wherever most subfamilies of the Austronesian family of languages have been spoken longest is probably the homeland where Austronesian languages originated.
(C) Taiwan is probably the homeland where Austronesian languages have been spoken longest.
(D) Austronesian-speaking peoples originated in the homeland where Austronesian languages have been spoken longest.
(E) Austronesian-speaking peoples probably originated in Taiwan and later migrated to other islands.

GO ON TO THE NEXT PAGE.

12. West: Of our company's three quality control inspectors, Haynes is clearly the worst. Of the appliances that were returned to us last year because of quality control defects, half were inspected by Haynes.

    Young: But Haynes inspects significantly more than half the appliances we sell each year.

    Young responds to West's argument by

    (A) contending that the argument presupposes what it is trying to prove
    (B) questioning the relevance of West's conclusion
    (C) disputing the accuracy of one of the argument's stated premises
    (D) arguing for a less extreme version of West's conclusion
    (E) denying one of the argument's presuppositions

13. While playing a game with a ball, both Emma and John carelessly ignored the danger their game posed to nearby objects. An errant throw by John struck and broke a neighbor's window. Because his throw broke the window, John, but not Emma, should be required to perform chores for the neighbor as compensation for the damage.

    Which one of the following conforms most closely to the principle illustrated above?

    (A) While looking after her neighbor's pets, Laura left the door to her neighbor's house unlocked. Fortunately, nothing bad happened as a result. But her neighbor should not trust Laura to look after her pets in the future.
    (B) Gerald hired Linda and Seung to move his furniture to a new residence. Linda and Seung carefully followed Gerald's instructions, but not all of the furniture fit in the moving truck. Gerald should still be required to pay Linda and Seung for the work they did.
    (C) Terry and Chris were racing their cars on a public street. Chris lost control of his car and struck a parked car. Chris, but not Terry, should be required to pay to repair the damage.
    (D) Alexis and Juan rented a boat for the afternoon. Because of improper use by the previous renter, the boat's engine malfunctioned during their excursion. The boat's owner should be required to refund Alexis's and Juan's rental fees.
    (E) Susan and Leland disregarded posted warnings in order to skate on a frozen pond. When the ice broke, Susan's ankle was injured. Susan cannot hold the pond's owners responsible for her injuries.

14. Psychology researchers observed that parents feel emotion while singing to their infants. The researchers hypothesized that this emotion noticeably affects the sound of the singing. To test this hypothesis the parents were recorded while singing to their infants and while singing with no infant present. They were instructed to make the two renditions as similar as possible. These recordings were then played for psychologists who had not observed the recordings being made. For 80 percent of the recordings, these psychologists were able to correctly identify, by listening alone, which recordings were of parents singing to their children. The researchers concluded that their hypothesis was correct.

    Which one of the following, if true, would most strengthen the researchers' reasoning?

    (A) A separate study by the same researchers found that parents feel more emotion when singing to their own children than when singing to other children.
    (B) Some, but not all, of the parents in the study realized that their song renditions were being recorded.
    (C) Parents displayed little emotion when singing with no child or adult present.
    (D) When a person feels emotion, that emotion provokes involuntary physiological responses that affect the vocal cords and lungs.
    (E) Most of the parents who participated in the study believed that the emotion they felt while singing to their infants affected their singing.

GO ON TO THE NEXT PAGE.

15. Many scholars claim that Shakespeare's portrayal of Richard III was extremely inaccurate, arguing that he derived that portrayal from propagandists opposed to Richard III. But these claims are irrelevant for appreciating Shakespeare's work. The character of Richard III as portrayed in Shakespeare's drama is fascinating and illuminating both aesthetically and morally, regardless of its relation to historical fact.

Which one of the following principles, if valid, most helps to justify the reasoning in the argument above?

(A) In historical drama, the aesthetic value of the work is not necessarily undermined by historical inaccuracies.

(B) In dealing with real people, dramatists should reflect their lives accurately.

(C) Shakespeare's historical importance puts him beyond the scope of all literary criticism.

(D) History is always told by propagandists from the winning side.

(E) Historical inaccuracies should be corrected only when they impugn the reputations of good people.

16. Voter: Our prime minister is evidently seeking a job at an international organization. Anyone seeking a job at an international organization would surely spend a lot of time traveling abroad, and our prime minister has spent more days abroad than at home so far this year.

Which one of the following arguments is most similar in its flawed reasoning to the voter's argument?

(A) Kao must be a golfer. Kao is planning to run for office, and most people who run for office play golf.

(B) Franklin will lose the coming election. The opposing candidate has better policy ideas and brings more relevant experience to the job.

(C) Ramirez is evidently able to control the traffic signals. Just now, as Ramirez approached the curb, the traffic signal changed from red to green.

(D) Thompson must be negotiating a personal loan. Thompson was at the bank yesterday, and people who are negotiating a personal loan go to the bank to meet with a loan agent.

(E) McKinsey must have committed a crime at some point. After all, despite extensive background checks no one has been able to show that McKinsey has never committed a crime.

17. It is pointless to debate the truth of the law of noncontradiction, a fundamental logical principle according to which two statements that contradict each other cannot both be true. For a debate to be productive, participants must hold some basic principles in common. But the principles held in common in a debate over the law of noncontradiction would be much less certain than that law, so it matters little whether the law of noncontradiction can be defended on the basis of those principles.

Which one of the following most accurately expresses the overall conclusion drawn in the argument?

(A) It is pointless to debate the truth of the law of noncontradiction.

(B) Statements that contradict each other cannot both be true.

(C) The participants in a productive debate must hold at least some basic principles in common.

(D) The law of noncontradiction is a principle that the participants in a productive debate must hold in common.

(E) Any principles that could be used to defend the law of noncontradiction are less certain than it is.

18. Pundit: For many high school graduates, attending a university would be of no help in getting a corporate job. The attributes corporations value most in potential employees are initiative, flexibility, and the ability to solve practical problems. Many new high school graduates have these attributes already.

The pundit's argument is most vulnerable to criticism on the grounds that it

(A) fails to establish that university graduates do not have initiative, flexibility, and the ability to solve practical problems

(B) overlooks the possibility that corporations may require an attribute that potential employees can obtain only by attending a university

(C) provides no justification for the presumption that corporations only hire employees who have initiative, flexibility, and the ability to solve practical problems

(D) takes for granted that the only reason that high school graduates go on to attend university is to improve their job prospects

(E) takes for granted that initiative, flexibility, and the ability to solve practical problems are attributes that can be acquired through study

GO ON TO THE NEXT PAGE.

19. Archaeologist: Neanderthals, a human-like species living 60,000 years ago, probably preserved meat by smoking it. Burnt lichen and grass have been found in many Neanderthal fireplaces. A fire of lichen and grass produces a lot of smoke but does not produce nearly as much heat or light as a wood fire.

Which one of the following, if true, would most weaken the archaeologist's argument?

(A) In close proximity to the fireplaces with lichen and grass are other fireplaces that, evidence suggests, burned material that produced more heat than smoke.
(B) In the region containing the Neanderthal fireplaces in which lichen and grass were burnt, no plants that could be burned more effectively to produce heat or light were available 60,000 years ago.
(C) Some of the fireplaces containing burnt lichen are in regions in which lichen is not believed to have been plentiful and so would have had to have been brought in from some distance.
(D) There is clear evidence that at least some groups of Neanderthals living more recently than 60,000 years ago developed methods of preserving meat other than smoking it.
(E) The ability to preserve meat through smoking would have made the Neanderthal humans less vulnerable to poor periods of hunting.

20. Edgar: Some of the pumps supplying water to our region have been ordered shut down in order to protect a species of small fish. But it is absurd to inconvenience thousands of people for the sake of something so inconsequential.

Rafaela: You're missing the point. The threat to that fish species is a sign of a very serious threat to our water supply.

The dialogue provides the most support for the claim that Edgar and Rafaela disagree over whether

(A) shutting down the pumps will actually inconvenience a large number of people
(B) the survival of the fish species is the only reason for shutting down the pumps
(C) species of small fish are inconsequential
(D) the order to shut down the pumps was legal
(E) shutting down the pumps will be sufficient to protect the fish species

21. Only engineering is capable of analyzing the nature of a machine in terms of the successful working of the whole; physics and chemistry determine the material conditions necessary for this success, but cannot express the notion of purpose. Similarly, only physiology can analyze the nature of an organism in terms of organs' roles in the body's healthy functioning. Physics and chemistry cannot ascertain by themselves any of these operational principles.

Which one of the following is an assumption required by the analogy?

(A) The functioning of the human organism is machine-like in nature.
(B) Physics and chemistry determine the material conditions required for good physiological functioning.
(C) The notion of purpose used by engineers to judge the success of machinery has an analog in organisms.
(D) Physiology as a science is largely independent of physics and chemistry.
(E) Biological processes are irreducible to mechanical or chemical processes.

GO ON TO THE NEXT PAGE.

22. After a hepadnavirus inserts itself into a chromosome of an animal, fragments of the virus are passed on to all of that animal's descendants. A hepadnavirus fragment is present in a chromosome of the zebra finch and in precisely the same location in a corresponding chromosome of the dark-eyed junco. The fact that these two bird species diverged from each other about 25 million years ago therefore means that the hepadnavirus is at least 25 million years old.

Which one of the following, if true, most strengthens the argument?

(A) Viruses can affect the evolution of an organism and can thereby influence the likelihood of their diverging into two species.

(B) The chromosomes of the zebra finch and the dark-eyed junco contain fragments of no virus other than the hepadnavirus.

(C) When a virus inserts itself into an animal's chromosome, the insertion occurs at a random spot.

(D) Many bird species other than the zebra finch and the dark-eyed junco contain fragments of the hepadnavirus.

(E) The presence of a hepadnavirus in an animal species does not affect the likelihood of that species' survival.

23. The diet of *Heliothis subflexa* caterpillars consists entirely of fruit from plants of the genus *Physalis*. These fruit do not contain linolenic acid, which is necessary to the growth and maturation of many insects other than *H. subflexa*. Linolenic acid in an insect's diet is also necessary for the production of a chemical called volicitin. While most caterpillar species have volicitin in their saliva, *H. subflexa* does not.

Which one of the following can be properly inferred from the statements above?

(A) *H. subflexa* caterpillars synthesize linolenic acid within their bodies.

(B) Most species of caterpillar have sources of linolenic acid in their diets.

(C) Any caterpillar that has linolenic acid in its diet has volicitin in its saliva.

(D) A food source containing linolenic acid would be poisonous to *H. subflexa* caterpillars.

(E) No caterpillars other than *H. subflexa* eat fruit from plants of the genus *Physalis*.

GO ON TO THE NEXT PAGE.

24. Politician: Democracy requires that there be no restrictions on the ability of citizens to share their ideas freely, without fear of reprisal. Therefore the right to have private conversations, unmonitored by the government, is essential to democracy. For a government to monitor conversations on the Internet would thus be a setback for democracy.

Which one of the following most accurately describes the role played in the argument by the claim that democracy depends on the ability of citizens to share their ideas freely, without fear of reprisal?

(A) It is a claim for which no support is provided, and which is used to support only the argument's main conclusion.

(B) It is a claim for which no support is provided, and which is used to support a claim that is itself used to support the argument's main conclusion.

(C) It is a claim for which support is provided, and which is in turn used to support the argument's main conclusion.

(D) It is the argument's main conclusion and is inferred from two other statements in the argument, one of which is used to support the other.

(E) It is the argument's main conclusion and is inferred from two other statements in the argument, neither of which is used to support the other.

25. One way to compare chess-playing programs is to compare how they perform with fixed time limits per move. Given any two computers with which a chess-playing program is compatible, and given fixed time limits per move, such a program will have a better chance of winning on the faster computer. This is simply because the program will be able to examine more possible moves in the time allotted per move.

Which one of the following is most strongly supported by the information above?

(A) If one chess-playing program can examine more possible moves than a different chess-playing program run on the same computer under the same time constraints per move, the former program will have a better chance of winning than the latter.

(B) How fast a given computer is has no effect on which chess-playing computer programs can run on that computer.

(C) In general, the more moves a given chess-playing program is able to examine under given time constraints per move, the better the chances that program will win.

(D) If two different chess-playing programs are running on two different computers under the same time constraints per move, the program running on the faster computer will be able to examine more possible moves in the time allotted.

(E) If a chess-playing program is run on two different computers and is allotted more time to examine possible moves when running on the slow computer than when running on the fast computer, it will have an equal chance of winning on either computer.

## S T O P

IF YOU FINISH BEFORE TIME IS CALLED, YOU MAY CHECK YOUR WORK ON THIS SECTION ONLY.
DO NOT WORK ON ANY OTHER SECTION IN THE TEST.

Acknowledgment is made to the following sources from which material has been adapted for use in this test booklet:

Paul Clerkin and Beth McLendon, "Eileen Gray" in *Irish Architecture Online.* ©1997 by Archéire.

Paul Davies, John G. Robb, and Dave Ladbrook, "Woodland Clearance in the Mesolithic: The Social Aspects" in *Antiquity.* ©2005 by *Antiquity* Publications, Ltd.

David Lewis, Letter in *The Law of Non-Contradiction.* Graham Priest, J.C. Beall, and Bradley Armour-Garb, eds. ©2004 by Oxford University Press.

Sandra Prior, "Does Muscle Memory Occur?" in EzineArticles.com. ©2007 by EzineArticles.com. http://ezinearticles.com/?Does-Muscle-Memory-Occur?&id=759493.

Tina Hesman Saey, "Muscles Can Remember Past Glory" in *ScienceNews.* ©2010 by Society for Science & the Public.

**Wait for the supervisor's instructions before you open the page to the topic.**
**Please print and sign your name and write the date in the designated spaces below.**

# Time: 35 Minutes

## General Directions

You will have 35 minutes in which to plan and write an essay on the topic inside. Read the topic and the accompanying directions carefully. You will probably find it best to spend a few minutes considering the topic and organizing your thoughts before you begin writing. In your essay, be sure to develop your ideas fully, leaving time, if possible, to review what you have written. **Do not write on a topic other than the one specified. Writing on a topic of your own choice is not acceptable.**

No special knowledge is required or expected for this writing exercise. Law schools are interested in the reasoning, clarity, organization, language usage, and writing mechanics displayed in your essay. How well you write is more important than how much you write.

Confine your essay to the blocked, lined area on the front and back of the separate Writing Sample Response Sheet. Only that area will be reproduced for law schools. Be sure that your writing is legible.

**Both this topic sheet and your response sheet must be turned in to the testing staff before you leave the room.**

| Topic Code | Print Your Full Name Here | | |
|---|---|---|---|
| | Last | First | M.I. |
| **133273** | | | |

| Date | Sign Your Name Here |
|---|---|
| /    / | |

# Scratch Paper
### Do not write your essay in this space.

# LSAT® Writing Sample Topic

**Directions:** The scenario presented below describes two choices, either one of which can be supported on the basis of the information given. Your essay should consider both choices and argue for one over the other, based on the two specified criteria and the facts provided. There is no "right" or "wrong" choice: a reasonable argument can be made for either.

Stonewall Construction is deciding which of two upcoming construction projects to bid on—resurfacing Hilltop Road or expanding Carlene Boulevard. Since Stonewall cannot fulfill both contracts at the same time and bids constitute binding commitments, Stonewall can only bid on one of them. Using the facts below, write an essay in which you argue for bidding on one project over the other based on the following two criteria:

- Stonewall wants to enhance its reputation among potential clients.
- Stonewall wants to increase its capacity to take on bigger projects.

The Hilltop Road resurfacing is a small project. The potential profit is relatively low. With Stonewall's experience and resources, it is almost certain to win the contract, and it is highly likely to finish on time and within budget. Stonewall has an established reputation for finishing projects on time and within budget. Stonewall has specialized in small projects. Construction firms specializing in small projects find it increasingly difficult over time to win contracts for bigger projects. If the project is completed under budget, Stonewall will keep the extra money. If it is over budget, Stonewall must cover the additional costs. Stonewall will use any extra money to purchase additional heavy equipment.

The Carlene Boulevard expansion is a large project. The potential profit is much higher. It involves kinds of work Stonewall has not done before and would require it to expand its operation. Because of the overall nature of this project Stonewall believes it has a good chance of winning the contract. It is uncertain whether Stonewall can finish the project on time and within budget. Even if Stonewall exceeds time and budget constraints, it will gain valuable experience. If the project goes over budget, Stonewall will lose money.

WP-W133A

# Scratch Paper
## Do not write your essay in this space.

# COMPUTING YOUR SCORE

## Directions:

1. Use the Answer Key on the next page to check your answers.

2. Use the Scoring Worksheet below to compute your raw score.

3. Use the Score Conversion Chart to convert your raw score into the 120–180 scale.

---

### Scoring Worksheet

1. Enter the number of questions you answered correctly in each section.

|  | Number Correct |
|---|---|
| SECTION I................ | _____ |
| SECTION II............... | _____ |
| SECTION III.............. | _____ |
| SECTION IV ............. | _____ |

2. Enter the sum here: _____

**This is your Raw Score.**

---

### Conversion Chart
### For Converting Raw Score to the 120–180 LSAT Scaled Score
### LSAT Form 6LSN120

| Reported Score | Raw Score Lowest | Raw Score Highest |
|---|---|---|
| 180 | 99 | 101 |
| 179 | 98 | 98 |
| 178 | 97 | 97 |
| 177 | 96 | 96 |
| 176 | * | * |
| 175 | 95 | 95 |
| 174 | 94 | 94 |
| 173 | 93 | 93 |
| 172 | 92 | 92 |
| 171 | 91 | 91 |
| 170 | 89 | 90 |
| 169 | 88 | 88 |
| 168 | 87 | 87 |
| 167 | 85 | 86 |
| 166 | 84 | 84 |
| 165 | 83 | 83 |
| 164 | 81 | 82 |
| 163 | 79 | 80 |
| 162 | 78 | 78 |
| 161 | 76 | 77 |
| 160 | 74 | 75 |
| 159 | 72 | 73 |
| 158 | 71 | 71 |
| 157 | 69 | 70 |
| 156 | 67 | 68 |
| 155 | 65 | 66 |
| 154 | 63 | 64 |
| 153 | 61 | 62 |
| 152 | 59 | 60 |
| 151 | 58 | 58 |
| 150 | 56 | 57 |
| 149 | 54 | 55 |
| 148 | 52 | 53 |
| 147 | 50 | 51 |
| 146 | 49 | 49 |
| 145 | 47 | 48 |
| 144 | 45 | 46 |
| 143 | 44 | 44 |
| 142 | 42 | 43 |
| 141 | 41 | 41 |
| 140 | 39 | 40 |
| 139 | 38 | 38 |
| 138 | 36 | 37 |
| 137 | 35 | 35 |
| 136 | 33 | 34 |
| 135 | 32 | 32 |
| 134 | 31 | 31 |
| 133 | 29 | 30 |
| 132 | 28 | 28 |
| 131 | 27 | 27 |
| 130 | 26 | 26 |
| 129 | 25 | 25 |
| 128 | 24 | 24 |
| 127 | 23 | 23 |
| 126 | 22 | 22 |
| 125 | 21 | 21 |
| 124 | 20 | 20 |
| 123 | 19 | 19 |
| 122 | 18 | 18 |
| 121 | * | * |
| 120 | 0 | 17 |

*There is no raw score that will produce this scaled score for this form.

# ANSWER KEY

## SECTION I

| | | | | | | | |
|---|---|---|---|---|---|---|---|
| 1. | C | 8. | E | 15. | A | 22. | E |
| 2. | E | 9. | B | 16. | B | 23. | D |
| 3. | D | 10. | C | 17. | C | 24. | B |
| 4. | D | 11. | C | 18. | A | 25. | A |
| 5. | B | 12. | A | 19. | D | 26. | E |
| 6. | B | 13. | E | 20. | D | | |
| 7. | A | 14. | E | 21. | E | | |

## SECTION II

| | | | | | | | |
|---|---|---|---|---|---|---|---|
| 1. | C | 8. | B | 15. | B | 22. | E |
| 2. | B | 9. | E | 16. | B | 23. | B |
| 3. | A | 10. | E | 17. | E | 24. | C |
| 4. | C | 11. | C | 18. | D | 25. | E |
| 5. | D | 12. | A | 19. | D | 26. | A |
| 6. | D | 13. | B | 20. | A | 27. | C |
| 7. | E | 14. | C | 21. | A | | |

## SECTION III

| | | | | | | | |
|---|---|---|---|---|---|---|---|
| 1. | B | 8. | D | 15. | A | 22. | C |
| 2. | C | 9. | D | 16. | C | 23. | C |
| 3. | A | 10. | E | 17. | D | | |
| 4. | B | 11. | B | 18. | D | | |
| 5. | D | 12. | A | 19. | E | | |
| 6. | E | 13. | A | 20. | A | | |
| 7. | C | 14. | B | 21. | C | | |

## SECTION IV

| | | | | | | | |
|---|---|---|---|---|---|---|---|
| 1. | D | 8. | B | 15. | A | 22. | C |
| 2. | A | 9. | A | 16. | D | 23. | B |
| 3. | D | 10. | A | 17. | A | 24. | B |
| 4. | A | 11. | E | 18. | B | 25. | C |
| 5. | D | 12. | E | 19. | B | | |
| 6. | B | 13. | C | 20. | B | | |
| 7. | D | 14. | D | 21. | C | | |

# LSAT® **PREP TOOLS**

# The Official LSAT SuperPrep II™

SuperPrep II contains everything you need to prepare for the LSAT—a guide to all three LSAT question types, three actual LSATs, explanations for all questions in the three practice tests, answer keys, writing samples, and score-conversion tables, plus invaluable test-taking instructions to help with pacing and timing. SuperPrep has long been our most comprehensive LSAT preparation book, and SuperPrep II is even better. The practice tests in SuperPrep II are PrepTest 62 (December 2010 LSAT), PrepTest 63 (June 2011 LSAT), and one test that has never before been disclosed.

With this book you can

- Practice on genuine LSAT questions
- Review explanations for right and wrong answers
- Target specific categories for intensive review
- Simulate actual LSAT conditions

LSAC sets the standard for LSAT prep—and SuperPrep II raises the bar!

**Available at your favorite bookseller.**

LSAC.org